3384 6048

P9-DNX-950

Bulgaria

Second Edition

STEVEN OTFINOSKI

■✓®
Facts On File, Inc.

Nations in Transition: Bulgaria, Second Edition

Facts On File, Inc.
132 West 31st Street
New York NY 10001

Library of Congress Cataloging-in-Publication Data

Otfinoski, Steven.
  Bulgaria / Steven Otfinoski. — 2nd ed.
    p. cm. — (Nations in transition)
  Includes bibliographical references and index.
  ISBN 0-8160-5116-X
  1. Bulgaria—History—1990—Juvenile literature. I. Title. II. Series.
  DR93.42.O86 2004
  949.903'2—dc22   2004043274

Facts On File books are available at special discounts when purchased in bulk quantities for businesses, associations, institutions, or sales promotions. Please call our Special Sales Department in New York at (212) 967-8800 or (800) 322-8755.

You can find Facts On File on the World Wide Web at
http://www.factsonfile.com

Text design by Erika K. Arroyo
Cover design by Nora Wertz
Maps by Dale Williams

Printed in the United States of America

MP FOF 10 9 8 7 6 5 4 3 2 1

This book is printed on acid-free paper.

To Elena Atanassova and
all the other young people of Bulgaria,
at home and abroad, who care
about their country and its future

CONTENTS

NOTE ON PRONUNCIATIONS

Throughout the text, pronunciations are given for Bulgarian words and names, but not for terms in Russian or other foreign languages.

Following is a list of symbols or letter combinations used for the vowel sounds:

a—as in Sar*a*h
o—as in sh*o*t
oo—as in j*u*bilee
e—as in *e*lephant
i—as in sh*e*
u—as in g*u*ts
ei—as in n*ei*ghbor
ai—as in *e*ye

For some consonants:

j—as in de*j*a vu
dj—as in *J*ack

Syllable that is stressed is in uppercase letters.

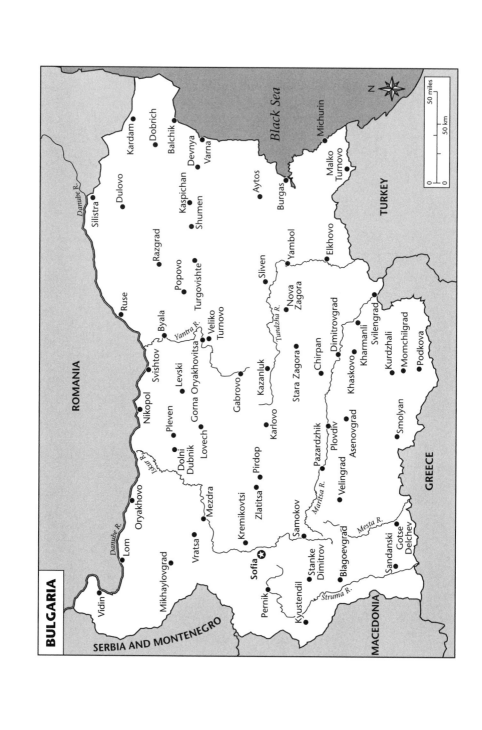

INTRODUCTION

On a warm Saturday in August 1999, hundreds of curious spectators gathered in Batenberg Square in Bulgaria's capital of Sofia (SO-fi-ya). They
came to watch a demolition crew blow up one of the city's most promi-
nent landmarks. The destruction of the massive white-marble mausoleum
was not just another example of urban renewal in post-independent Bulgaria. This last resting place of the country's first Communist leader,
Georgi Dimitrov (ge-OR-gi di-mi-TROF) (1882–1949), was seen, in the
words of Prime Minister Ivan Kostov (I-VAN KOS-tof) (b. 1949), as a
"symbol of autocratic totalitarian power." Dimitrov's mummified body
was gone, removed from the tomb and burned in 1990, but the mausoleum that memorialized him still stood as an ugly reminder of the Communist past.

Not everyone gathered in the large square was in favor of the demolition. Members of the Socialist Party, who were formerly members of the
very Communist Party that Kostov was vilifying, looked up grimly at the
government officials watching the spectacle from a nearby roof. They saw
Kostov's actions as stemming from political motivations rather than
moral ones. According to some polls, as many as two-thirds of the Bulgarian people also disapproved of the building's razing.

After much waiting, the 1,323 pounds (600 kilograms) of explosives
were detonated. Buildings shook. The windows of neighboring government offices shattered. But when the dust and smoke cleared, the 4.9-foot
(1.5-meter)-thick walls of the Dimitrov mausoleum were still standing.
The crowd in the square jeered and cheered as the government officials
on the rooftop fidgeted nervously.

More explosives were packed into the walls and detonated. The mausoleum again refused to collapse. The Socialists shouted to the embarrassed officials that they would never find "enough ammunition to destroy our ideas."

The next day Prime Minister Kostov ordered bulldozers to be sent in to raze the building. After a week of concerted effort, the demolition gangs finally brought down Dimitrov's tomb. But by then it was too late. Instead of demonstrating its strength in the face of tyranny, the government had only displayed its own ineffectualness to the world.

The resilience of the Communists was stronger than the walls of the massive memorial. Even after their government's collapse in 1989, the Communists had remained in charge. As the "Socialist Party," their members managed to regain power twice in national elections in the 1990s, slowing the transition to a democratic, free-market system almost to a standstill. In their second tenure (1994–97), they managed to lead Bulgaria further down the path of economic ruin and near political chaos.

But the word *transition* has more than one meaning for this struggling Balkan nation. Emerging from Communist domination is only one transition Bulgaria must make at the dawn of the 21st century. One of Europe's poorest countries, it is still in the midst of making the larger transition from centuries of political, economic, and social backwardness to modern nationhood. "The sense that Bulgaria needed to do fifty years' worth of catching up made the transition to democracy even harder," observed writer Pamela Mitova (MI-to-va).

The Union of Democratic Forces (UDF) that had taken power in 1997 was only marginally more effective. While they were able to destroy a Communist symbol, they could not destroy the debilitating effects of the system it represented. More to the point, they failed to build a new economic system that would bring stability and relief to a long-suffering people. Within two years of the spectacle in Batenberg Square, Kostov and his government would themselves be voted out of office and replaced by the man who had ruled Bulgaria before Dimitrov and the Communists had seized control. An important link with a happier, pre-Soviet past, Simeon Saxe-Coburg, previously known as King Simeon II, now has his chance to take Bulgaria into a better future.

The Bulgarians have little to compare this future to. They have spent most of the past 600 years under the yoke of two masters—the Turks, whom they hated, and the Russians, whom they embraced as liberators. It was the Russians who freed Bulgaria from the harsh rule of the Ottoman Turks in 1878, but who then made the Bulgarians their vassals.

Bulgaria's relationship with the Soviet Union during the 40 years of Soviet domination was a unique one. Until the 1980s, dissent against the Communist regime was practically nonexistent, although there was plenty to dissent against. Half a century of Communist rule had disrupted traditions, broken the people's spirit, and polluted their once pristine land. On the other hand, the Soviets brought Bulgaria into the 20th century, industrialized the country, improved agriculture, and boosted the standard of living for millions of people.

The most loyal of the Soviet satellite countries, Bulgaria remained as remote to most Westerners as the moon. "The average European knows only that Bulgaria was Moscow's most loyal satellite," noted Bulgarian historian Bojidar Dimitrov (bo-ji-DAR di-mi-TROF), "that its military industry was selling weapons all over the globe, and that it looked as if it had something to do with drug trafficking and the attempt to assassinate the Pope."

Its very isolation from Western Europe and the United States has made Bulgaria all the more reluctant to embrace Western ways, although young Bulgarians are as attracted to the West, as are the youth of Poland, Hungary, and the Czech Republic.

"It's a question of where we are," Bulgarian filmmaker Vladimir Andreev (vla-di-MIR an-DRE-ef) has said. "Geographically we're in Europe, but there is quite a strong tendency, as in Russia, to believe that we're something special with our own history and problems, and that the principles of Europe can't be exactly implanted here."

That Bulgaria is indeed something special is only beginning to be recognized by the West. As its ancient cities, resilient people, and colorful folk arts and music are being discovered by the West, Westerners are learning who the Bulgarians are, and the crisis they are facing becomes more compelling.

NATIONAL CHARACTER

"We Bulgarians are such people—we suffer and do nothing." With these words Maria Vaseva (VA-se-va), an unemployed electronics specialist, sums up what she considers the dark side of the Bulgarian national character. At the same time, this deep strain of stoicism has helped this Balkan country survive countless foreign invasions and occupations.

Apathy can be seen as a national malaise, particularly in the 13 years since the collapse of communism. But if the Bulgarians' tolerance for oppression seems high, so is their love of work, thoughtfulness to others, and love of people, especially family.

Family is everything to Bulgarians. They lavish care on their children, take in the elderly, and are close to brothers, sisters, and cousins. Most Bulgarians believe in hard work, and they are always busy. As one old Bulgarian proverb states: "Work left for later is finished by the Devil."

While work is important, so is play. Bulgarians of all classes love to sing and dance. Telling stories and jokes is a national pastime and conversation is as natural as breathing. Nowhere is this more apparent than on a Bulgarian train. Perfect strangers who start a journey in the same railroad car often end up telling each other their life story before arriving at their destination.

Although long considered in the backwater of Europe, Bulgarians pride themselves on being well educated. Reading is a favorite pastime, whether it be newspapers, magazines, or books.

While religion is important to Bulgarians, faith for many does not run deep. Religion is part of their national spirit, and their allegiance to

Small Country, Mixed Geography

Bulgaria is located in southeastern Europe on the Balkan Peninsula, which it shares with Romania, the republics of the former Yugoslavia, Albania, Greece, and European Turkey. It is a small country, a little bigger than the state of Tennessee, with population of some 7.5 million. About 84 percent of the population is Bulgarian, while another 10 percent are ethnic Turks who have lived here for hundreds of years. The

the Bulgarian Orthodox Church is as much an expression of fervent patriotism as it is of religious conviction.

Good and bad, the national character of the Bulgarians has both held them back from new challenges and sustained them when faced with seemingly insurmountable ones.

The joy of living, even in hard times, is captured in the smile of this peasant woman as she herds her sheep. The Bulgarian national character is a curious mixture of optimism and apathy. (Courtesy Library of Congress)

remaining 6 percent of people are mostly Roma (Gypsies), Armenians, Russians, Macedonians, and Greeks.

The Roma are a nomadic people originally from India who live throughout Europe. The Armenians, Russians, and Greeks have immigrated here from their respective homelands. The Macedonians are descendants of a once great country located south of Bulgaria that was the home of the conqueror Alexander the Great (356–323 B.C.). Over the centuries, Macedonia was absorbed by Bulgaria, Greece, and the former Yugoslavia. It again became an independent republic in 1991.

Bulgaria is bounded to the north by Romania, to the east by the Black Sea, which provides it with a 175-mile (282-kilometer) coast-

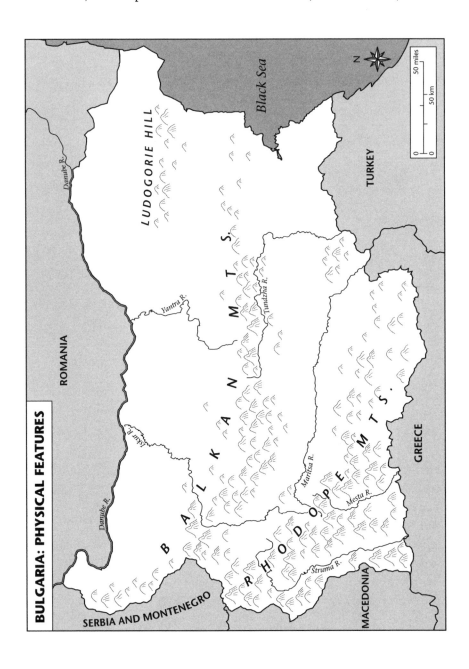

line, to the south by Greece and Turkey, and on the west by Serbia and Macedonia.

Although small, Bulgaria has a surprising variety of land forms. More than two-thirds of the country is covered with plains and plateaus, while nearly a quarter of the remaining land is mountainous. Bulgaria's mountains have been both a blessing and a curse. They have isolated villages, cutting them off from the rest of the world for centuries. They have also provided Bulgarian freedom fighters through history with a safe haven from the countless invaders who have attacked and occupied their land. From north to south, there are four main geographical regions. The Danube River, which marks most of its northern border with Romania, forms a huge plateau that extends south to the Balkan Mountains. The Danube, Europe's second-longest river, is a far cry from "the beautiful blue Danube" of the famous Strauss waltz. It is more yellow than blue from silt, sand, and industrial pollution. Yet the Danubian Plateau contains Bulgaria's most fertile soil, which produces wheat, corn, sugar beets, tobacco, and sunflowers.

The Balkan Mountains, running from east to west, nearly slice the country in half. These ancient peaks give the entire peninsula its name, and the Bulgarians refer to them as "Stara Planina" (STA-ra pla-ni-NA) or "Old Mountains." They are composed of granite and crystalline rock and contain deposits of some minerals, although they are better known for the timber of their thick forests.

Below the Balkans are the Lowlands and Transitional Mountains with more fertile valleys, including the Valley of Roses, where one of Bulgaria's most famous exports, rose oil, is made (see sidebar, chapter 6).

Further south, to the west, marking Bulgaria's border with Greece, are the Rhodope (ro-DO-pi) Mountains, fabled in Bulgarian folklore and song. They are rich in timber and minerals and contain the country's highest point, Musala (moo-sa-LA) Peak, which rises 9,596 feet (2,925 m).

Equally legendary is the Black Sea to the east, named for the dark hue created by storm clouds and fog in the winter, or for the dark demons that once inhabited its shores, according to Bulgarian folklore. But most of the year, the Black Sea is bright and crystal clear. In the summer months, it attracts 1.5 million vacationers who enjoy its sunny beaches and comfortable resorts. It remains the center of Bulgaria's thriving tourist industry.

Bulgaria's varied terrain creates a wide range of climactic conditions. Summers in the north tend to be humid; in the south, dry. Most of the country enjoys mildly cold winters and the only heavy snowfall is in the mountain regions.

Bulgaria is plagued by one natural disaster—earthquakes. Sixteen major quakes have struck in this century, most of them in the north and the west Rhodopes.

Plant and Animal Life

Only about 29 percent of Bulgaria is forested, including the Balkan and Rhodope Mountains. Conifers, beech, and oak trees dominate in the Rhodopes. Little wildlife is found outside the mountain zones, where wolves, elks, foxes, wild cats, badgers, and bears live. Some of these creatures are endangered by a shrinking habitat, especially bears.

The Vitosha National Park near Sofia provides a shelter for many mammals, birds, and a wide variety of butterflies. Established in 1934, the park encompasses all of Vitosha Mountain. The National Trust EcoFund of Bulgaria is committed to increasing the numbers of nature preserves in this highly urbanized country.

Land of Contrasts

Like its geography, Bulgaria's culture is full of contrasts. The ancient and the modern stand side by side. In Sofia, the remains of a tower built nearly 2,000 years ago by the Romans sits in the basement of a modern department store. The cab that takes young people to Eddy's Tex-Mex Diner, one of the capital's hottest nightspots, may have its hood adorned with a collar of beads meant to ward off the evil eye. One of the most celebrated of contemporary Bulgarians is the artist Christo (HRI-sto), who creates strange artworks by wrapping monuments, buildings, and natural landscapes with plastics and fabrics.

Poor in many things, Bulgaria is a land rich in physical beauty, history, culture, and the spirit of its people. Hopefully, the difficult transitions it is now facing will not rob it of these riches.

NOTES

p. ix "'symbol of autocratic totalitarian power.'" BBC News Online Network. Available on-line. URL: http://news.bbc.co.uk/1/hi/world/europe/427068.stm. Downloaded on October 19, 2003.

p. x "'enough ammunition to destroy our ideas.'" BBC News Online. See above.

p. x "'The sense that Bulgaria needed . . .'" Pamela Mitova, *Bulgaria: A Country Study* (Washington, D.C.: Library of Congress, 1993), p. 61.

p. xi "'The average European . . .'" *New York Times*, Travel Section, June 23, 1996, p. 17.

p. xi "'It's a question of where we are . . .'" *New York Times*, April 28, 1995, p. A11.

p. xii "'We Bulgarians are such people . . .'" Alison Smale, "Bulgarians Fearful of Future," Associated Press News Service, July 21, 1996. CD NewsBank.

p. xii "'Work left for later . . .'" Kirilka Stavreva, *Bulgaria* (New York: Marshall Cavendish, 1997), p. 47.

PART I
History

1
IN THE POWDER
KEG OF EUROPE
(PREHISTORY TO 1919)

Few lands in Europe have been inhabited longer than Bulgaria. Archaeologists have found evidence of cave dwellers living in parts of the country as far back as perhaps 100,000 years ago. In all that time, the people of this rugged land have known little peace. Bulgaria's history, like that of its neighbors on the Balkan Peninsula, is riddled with bloodshed, violence, and war that has often spread across the continent. It has earned the region the title the "Powder Keg of Europe."

Early Civilizations and Their Downfalls

The first people to establish a civilization in Bulgaria were the Thracians. They arrived from the north during the Bronze Age around 4000 B.C. The empire they established, called Thrace, included not only present-day Bulgaria but most of the Balkan Peninsula and Romania.

The Greek historian Herodotus (ca. 484–ca. 420 B.C.) described the Thracians as "the most numerous of peoples after the Indians [people of India]," commenting that "only their chronic disunity prevents them from being the most powerful of all nations." The Thracians were, in fact, a people of curious contrasts. They loved music, literature, and philosophy.

They also loved war and killed and looted their neighbors with a savage ferocity. Yet they seemed to have gotten along with the Greeks, their neighbors to the south, and allowed them to build trading centers along their coastline on the Black Sea.

The Macedonians, who lived to the north, conquered Thrace in the fourth century B.C. under the strong leadership of Philip II (382–336 B.C.). Philip's son, Alexander the Great, ruled the Thracians until his early death, when the empire he had built crumbled. Within the next two centuries, the Romans invaded Thrace and made it a part of their vast empire. The Thracians were subjugated by the Romans, and many of them were enslaved. Their civilization vanished into the mists of history, but the name Thrace remained on the map of Europe into the 20th century as a geographic section of the Balkans.

In A.D. 330 the Roman emperor Constantine the Great (ca. 288–337) moved his capital from Rome to Byzantium, one of the cities that the Thracians let the Greeks establish on the Bosporus Strait, which connects the Black Sea and the Sea of Marmara. The city's name was changed to Constantinople in the emperor's honor. In 395 the Roman Empire split in two, with the West Roman Empire still centered in Rome and the East Roman Empire in Constantinople. The western empire went into decline, its collapse hastened by barbarian invasions from the north, but the eastern empire, known as the Byzantine Empire, expanded and flourished.

While these events were taking place, two new peoples moved into what is now Bulgaria. The Slavs were a peaceful, farming people who came from southern Poland and Russia in the sixth century. Less than a century later, their peace was threatened by fierce warriors called Bulgars (BOOL-gars), who thundered across the plains of Central Asia on horseback. The word Bulgar comes from an Old Turkic word that means "one of mixed nationality." As fierce as they were, the Bulgars came under the civilizing influence of the Slavs, and they gradually became assimilated into Slavic culture. Out of this commingling of the two groups, a new people were born—the Bulgarians.

The First and Second Bulgarian Kingdoms

Bulgar aggressiveness and Slavic order helped the Bulgarians form a new civilization of their own. In 681 Bulgar Khan (HAN), or Prince,

SIMEON I (CA. 863–927, REIGNED 893–927)

If Bulgaria ever had a "golden age," it was surely under the rule of Simeon I, considered one of his country's greatest monarchs. Warrior lord, patron of the arts, and religious leader, Simeon was a superb national leader in every way.

Christianity, although a relatively new religion in Bulgaria, ran deep in his blood. His father, Boris I (reigned 852–889), gave up his throne to become a monk, only to see his elder son, Vladimir (vla-di-MIR), turn his back on the church and attempt to revive Bulgaria's pagan gods. Boris returned from his monastery, deposed Vladimir, and made his younger son, Simeon, king.

Simeon quickly proved himself a strong leader. He went to war against his country's main rival in the region, the Byzantine Empire, defeated it soundly, and came close to taking its capital, Constantinople. He conquered Serbia and vanquished the dreaded warrior tribe the Magyars, driving them into present-day Hungary.

Simeon embraced the Eastern Orthodox Church,* rather than the Roman Catholic Church, determining the religious path of his people for the next two millennia. He established a national church, the Bulgarian Orthodox Church, and made the archbishop of Bulgaria a patriarch, the highest ranking bishop in this new church. This church remains the largest religious group in Bulgaria to this day.

A dedicated scholar, Simeon encouraged and supported the translation of Greek literature into the Slavonic language of the church. The arts, especially literature, reached new heights during his reign.

In 925, two years before his death, Simeon named himself czar of all the Bulgars and autocrat of the Greeks. The First Bulgarian Kingdom, however, did not survive him by long. His son and successor, Peter, did not have his strengths, and the empire quickly fell apart under the weight of foreign and internal turmoil.

---

*The eastern and western Christian churches split in 1054, after drifting apart for several centuries. The Eastern Orthodox Church was a federation of churches united by common beliefs but independent in each nation or region. The Roman Catholic Church was united under the authority of the pope in Rome.

Asparuhk (as-pa-ROOHK) (reigned 680–701) broke with the Byzantine Empire, which had previously dominated his people, and established the First Bulgarian Kingdom. Over the next two centuries, the kingdom stretched from Macedonia in the north to Albania and Serbia in the west and parts of the Byzantine Empire in the east. It reached its apex under the wise and firm rule of Simeon I (see boxed biography), who came to power in 893 and gave himself the title of czar, a Slavic version of "Caesar." Simeon ushered in a golden age of art, literature, and trade.

The kingdom, however, was short-lived. By 1018 the larger Byzantine Empire swallowed up the Bulgarian Kingdom after a series of debilitating wars. Internal conflicts and new barbarian invasions weakened the empire. By 1186 the Bulgarians were able to break free again and establish the Second Bulgarian Kingdom under Ivan I. The kingdom grew and prospered under Ivan's son Czar Kaloyan (ka-lo-YAN) (reigned 1197–1207) and his grandson Ivan II (reigned 1218–41), who came to control all of the Balkan Peninsula, except for Greece.

Bulgarian culture and influence reached its second high watermark in the 13th century. Many centuries would pass before the Bulgarians would again enjoy such freedom and happiness.

In the Grip of the Ottoman Turks

By the early 1300s, a new conqueror emerged out of central Asia. The Ottoman Turks were fierce nomadic warriors, who also had a genius for governing the peoples they conquered. From their Middle Eastern base they moved westward into Christian Europe. They gradually conquered the Byzantine Empire and the regions surrounding it, including the Balkans. By the end of the century, they had taken over all of Bulgaria. In 1453 the Turks broke the Byzantine stronghold at Constantinople and made the city the headquarters of their growing empire. Today this city is known as Istanbul.

Ottoman supremacy in Bulgaria was unchallenged and would remain so for the next 500 years. Thousands of Turks poured into Bulgaria and brought with them their government, culture, and Muslim religion. By the end of the 16th century, two-thirds of the population of Sofia, the capital, was Turkish.

The Bulgarians who were willing to convert to the Muslim religion were dealt with fairly, even kindly by the Turks. Those that refused to give up Christianity and their national identity were dealt with harshly. When met by resistance, the Turks were merciless. Entire villages and towns that fought back were wiped out. Land and property of local farmers were seized. Heavy taxes were imposed on the populace. The Bulgarians countered with a series of revolts—in the 1590s, the 1680s, and the 1730s. Each rebellion was crushed by the Turks, but a national movement for independence took root and grew.

One of the leaders of the cause of Bulgarian nationalism was a monk, Father Paisiy (pa-I-si) Khilendarski (1722–73), who lived in the monastery of Hilendar on Mount Athos in Macedonia. In 1762 he wrote the first literary work in the modern Bulgarian language, *History of Slavo-Bulgarians*. It would circulate among the populace for nearly a hundred years in manuscript form before being published, fueling the fires of patriotism.

As the Turkish state was weakened by numerous wars with its enemies, more freedom was granted to the Bulgarians to keep them content and less rebellious. Local schools teaching in the Bulgarian language opened, the Bulgarian Orthodox Church was revived, and new printing presses published Bulgarian books and newspapers.

But these social reforms only whetted the people's appetite for political autonomy. In April 1876 they staged what would be their last uprising against the Turks. Bulgarian farmers fought the well-armed Turkish army with crude homemade weapons. They fashioned cannons out of cherry trees lined with copper from the pipes of vats used to distill rose oil.

The uprising failed and this time Turkish reprisals were harsh. They destroyed some 100 villages and five monasteries. An estimated 30,000 people—men, women, and children—were massacred in what the international press darkly referred to as "the Bulgarian atrocities."

Januarius MacGahan (1844–78), an American war correspondent for the London *Daily News*, wrote this sobering account on entering the Bulgarian village of Batak (ba-TAK) after the Turks had finished with it:

> I could distinguish one slight skeletal form still enclosed in a chemise, the skull wrapped with a colored handkerchief, and the bony ankles encased in the embroidered footless stockings worn by Bulgarian girls. The ground was strewn with bones in every direction, where the dogs had carried them off to gnaw them at their leisure. At the distance of a hundred yards beneath us lay the town. As seen from our standpoint, it reminded one of the ruins of Herculaneum or Pompeii.

Independence—Of a Sort

Such scenes of slaughter shocked the world and sealed the fate of a decaying, tyrannical empire. Imperial Russia, anxious to expand its own sphere of influence, used the repression of the Balkan Slavs as an excuse to go to war against the Turks. During the Russo-Turkish War (1877–78), Russian troops marched in and enlisted Bulgarian patriots to fight with them. At the famed battle at the Shipka Pass, the Russians and Bulgarians were hopelessly outnumbered by Turkish troops, but they nonetheless took the day. Some 13,000 Turks died in the fighting, but only 5,500 Russians perished. After five centuries of Turkish rule, Bulgaria was liberated.

It was a historic moment that the Bulgarian people would never forget. The bond forged between Russians and Bulgarians at the Shipka Pass would survive two world wars and 40 years of Soviet domination.

The Russian victory in the Russo-Turkish War ended 500 years of Turkish rule in Bulgaria. Here Russian troops storm the city of Pleven, defended by the Turks in July 1877. After a four-month siege, the Turks signed an armistice. (Courtesy Library of Congress)

The Treaty of San Stefano in 1878 established Bulgaria as an autonomous republic within the Ottoman Empire, or what was left of it. But the major nations of western Europe had no intention of giving Russia a foothold in the Balkans. At a congress held in Berlin, Germany, later that year, the treaty was seriously revised and territory designated to be returned to Bulgaria was taken back, including Macedonia, which remained under Turkish rule. Bulgaria itself was divided into three parts, making national unity all but impossible. It was a bitter disappointment for the Bulgarians, the first of many they would experience in the coming years.

The Balkan Wars and World War I

A German prince, Ferdinand (1861–1948), was chosen to govern the country and was crowned its monarch in 1908. One of his first acts as czar was to declare Bulgaria fully independent from the Turks. But Bulgaria had been rapidly changing in the decades leading up to this moment. Under Ferdinand, this previously backward agricultural country had its first taste of industrialization. Between 1887 and 1911 the number of industrial plants in Bulgaria rose from 36 to 345. Bulgaria was slowly preparing to enter the 20th century.

Although the Ottoman Empire was "the Sick Man of Europe," according to the Western press, it was still a threat to change in the Balkans. In 1912 Bulgaria joined Greece, Serbia, and Montenegro* in a war to drive the Turks once and for all from European soil. The war was short and ended in utter defeat for the Turks, although they retained Constantinople for a time. The Bulgarians were rewarded with Thrace as a spoil of war but were denied Macedonia by their allies. They heedlessly declared war on Serbia, hoping to take Macedonia back by force.

In this Second Balkan War (1913), Bulgaria was hopelessly outnumbered. Greece, Romania, and Montenegro took the side of the Serbs. After less than a month of bloody fighting, the Bulgarians asked for a truce. In the Treaty of Bucharest, Bulgaria lost almost every inch of territory it had gained from the First Balkan War. Macedonia was divided up among the victors, with only a small corner going to Bulgaria.

---

*Serbia and Montenegro would both later become part of Yugoslavia.

Serbia was now the dominant country in the Balkans, and it wanted back the territories of Bosnia and Herzegovina, which were in the hands of the Austro-Hungarian Empire. When Archduke Francis Ferdinand (1863–1914), heir to the Austro-Hungarian throne, visited Bosnia in June 1914, he was assassinated by a Serb nationalist. Soon after, Austria-Hungary, backed by Germany, declared war on Serbia. Russia came to the aid of the Serbs, and World War I was under way.

At first, Bulgaria remained neutral, but in 1915 it sided with Germany and Austria-Hungary. The only other Balkan country to do so was Turkey. King Ferdinand's government hoped to regain its lost territory from the Serbs. The war was a devastating one for the Balkans, and the Bulgarian people protested against their country's participation. The Social Democratic Party, composed of Communists, supported this stance and gained valuable support from the people.

On September 28, 1918, Bulgaria surrendered and signed an armistice with the Allies—principally Great Britain, France, and the United

Dead soldiers are scattered across a bleak battlefield in the Balkans during World War I. Bulgaria's decision to join the Germans and Austrians in the war was a fatal one. (Courtesy Library of Congress)

States. When news of this reached Germany, one official said, "The war will end in four months, it cannot continue longer because the states will collapse." It ended in German defeat sooner than that. Bulgaria, under the Treaty of Neuilly, was forced to pay reparations to Serbia and its allies. It also lost more territory, this time to the newly formed nation of Yugoslavia, while Greece gained Bulgaria's outlet to the Aegean Sea. King Ferdinand, in disgrace, abdicated and his son, Boris, became king.

In three wars in just over four years, the Bulgarians had lost valuable territory, many lives, and all self-respect. The war-torn country was fraught with political turmoil and unrest. Terrorist groups struggled for control of the country. Many feared the government would break down completely and that anarchy would take over. But another devastating war would take its toll before Bulgaria would find a new kind of stability and peace under the heel of still another conqueror.

NOTES

p. 3 "'the most numerous of peoples . . .'" R. F. Hoddinott, *The Thracians* (New York: Thames and Hudson, 1981), p. 14.

p. 7 "I could distinguish one slight skeletal form . . ." Dale L. Walker, *Januarius MacGahan: The Life and Campaigns of an American War Correspondent* (Athens, Ohio: Ohio University Press, 1988), p. 178.

p. 11 "'The war will end . . .'" John Toland, *No Man's Land: 1918—The Last Year of the Great War* (New York: Doubleday, 1980), p. 449.

2

TERRORISM, WAR, AND STABILITY AT A PRICE (1919 TO 1985)

The end of World War I left Bulgaria in total disarray, both politically and economically. But there was hope for a new and better future. Out of the quagmire of quarreling political parties emerged the Bulgarian Agrarian National Union (BANU), which gained 28 percent of the vote in elections held in 1919. Once in power, the agrarians and their leader, Alexander Stambuliski (Stam-boo-LI-ski) (1879–1923), tried to reform the age-old landholding system and share the land and its wealth with the peasants. Stambuliski ended all attempts to regain lost territory that had led Bulgaria into three devastating wars and focused instead on domestic problems. He made secondary schooling compulsory for all Bulgarian children and supported a new progressive income tax.

Unfortunately, his policies made him as many enemies as they did friends. Urban workers felt neglected by the agrarians because they favored the peasant farmers, and large numbers of them joined the Communist Party. At the same time, Macedonian nationalists were angry with the government for abandoning the fight to regain their ancestral lands.

In 1923, Stambuliski's opponents staged a bloody coup. He was assassinated and his government overthrown. The new government, largely in the hands of the military, was right wing and extremely repressive. In 1924 it outlawed the Communist Party. In retaliation, the Soviet Union sent agents to Bulgaria to engage in acts of terrorism. One of the most brutal of these was the bombing of Sofia's Sveta Nedelia (Sve-TA ne-DE-lya) Cathedral in a plot to kill King Boris III (1894–1943). Boris was unharmed in the blast, but more than 100 others died.

A new, more tolerant leader, Andrei Liapchev (an-DREI LYAP-chev) (1866–1933), brought some stability to Bulgaria in the late 1920s. But before the country could benefit from his policies, the world economic depression reached Eastern Europe. In a short time, 200,000 workers were unemployed and the per capita income of the peasants dropped by 50 percent.

In Eastern Europe, fascism was on the rise, feeding off the frustrations of downtrodden peoples who wanted economic security and a sense of national self-respect. Liapchev was defeated in the election of 1931 and Zveno (zve-NO), a new political coalition that had the backing of fascist Italy, came to prominence. In 1934 Zveno seized the government in another coup.

King Boris Takes Over

Boris III felt the Zveno government would only bring more ruin to Bulgaria, and in 1935 he asserted his considerable power and created a royal dictatorship. Boris's authoritarian rule was no worse and probably better than that of any other faction in Bulgaria and brought a much-needed stability to the troubled nation. But it also weakened the country politically. When elections were held in 1938, Boris declared that only individuals without party affiliations could run for office.

But if the king could control events within his country, the world outside would not be so manageable. Nazi Germany saw Bulgaria as a key to the Balkans, and it began to exert its influence in the country economically by becoming one of its main trading partners.

As the world teetered on the brink of another major war, Boris struggled to remain neutral, but Germany and Italy, the Axis Powers, would not allow him to do so. Germany's promise of regained territory reawak-

Boris III stands tall in his military uniform. His royal dictatorship in the 1930s brought stability but politically weakened his country. When the Germans forced an alliance with Bulgaria in World War II, Boris did his best to keep his people out of the fighting and helped spare the lives of thousands of Bulgarian Jews. (Courtesy Library of Congress)

ened old nationalistic dreams, and the government clamored for an alliance. In March 1941, Bulgaria signed the Tripartite Pact with both Germany and Italy. The die was cast.

A Reluctant Ally

Despite its status as an ally, Bulgaria sent no soldiers to fight for the Axis Powers. Instead, the Germans used Bulgaria as their base of operations in fighting neighboring Greece and Yugoslavia, both of whom supported the Western Allies—the United States and Britain.

While Boris agreed to declare war on the Allies, he refused to break off diplomatic relations with the Soviet Union, which sided with the Allies after the Germans attacked it in 1941. Boris feared his own people would turn on him if they were forced to fight the country that was still seen by many Bulgarians as a liberator and friend.

There was another issue on which Bulgarians would not be coerced into action. Nazi leader Adolf Hitler declared that all Jews in Eastern Europe were to be detained and then sent to concentration camps. Boris and his government agreed to pass the anti-Semitic laws the Nazis foisted on them, but they were not prepared to act on them. Bulgaria's 50,000 Jews had lived there for centuries, as they had in many parts of Eastern Europe. Historian and Bulgarian-born Jew Michael Bar-Zohar recalled vividly the night in March 1943 when he and his family joined other Bulgarian Jews on what they thought would be their last journey:

> . . . we were ordered to pack a few belongings into a bag and get ready to be taken away by the police. . . . We can still describe the long trains of boxcars waiting for the Bulgarian Jews at the railway stations. We remember the crying, the despair, the terrible feeling of doom and impending death, and the ominous mention of "camps in Poland," which meant cruel annihilation.
>
> But we were not taken away. The boxcars left the stations, empty. We didn't know exactly what had happened, but the Jews of Bulgaria were saved at the very last minute.

In the end, it seemed, the Bulgarian people were not willing to have their friends and neighbors sent to an almost certain death. Politicians, religious leaders of the Bulgarian Orthodox Church, intellectuals, and members of the business community joined together to protest the deportation of Jews. Mass demonstrations ensued, and soon after the Bulgarian parliament revoked the anti-Semitic laws. Not one Bulgarian Jew went to a gas chamber during World War II, a record unmatched by any other country in Europe.

But Bulgaria did not escape from the war unscathed. The Allied Air Command heavily bombed the German-occupied country. By the war's end, 32,000 Bulgarians had lost their lives in the fighting.

In 1943 King Boris, who had done his best to cushion his people from the ravages of the war, died mysteriously after visiting Hitler in Berlin. To this day there is speculation that he was secretly murdered by either Hitler or Soviet agents. His successor was his six-year-old son, Simeon II

Six-year-old Simeon II plays with a toy tank during military maneuvers. Simeon would flee Bulgaria with his mother three years later when the Communists took over the government and abolished the monarchy. (Courtesy Library of Congress)

(see boxed biography, chapter 4). As the fortunes of war were shifting in the Allies' favor, Bulgaria tried to make peace with the United States and Britain. But in September 1944, during peace talks with these countries, the Soviet Union declared war on Bulgaria. Within days, Soviet troops overran the country.

The Soviet Union's Little Brother

At first the Communists seemed willing to share power with the other political parties in Bulgaria in a coalition called the Fatherland Front. But over the next two years, they gradually took control of the front and won more than half the seats in the National Assembly in elections held in the fall of 1946. Georgi Dimitrov, a Communist trained by Russian leader Joseph Stalin, became prime minister in the new government. Those who opposed the Communist government were arrested, put on trial, convicted, and either executed or sent to prison.

The Communists set out to eradicate totally the Agrarian Union, their most serious rival for power. Agrarian leader Nikola Petkov (ni-KO-la pet-KOF) received support and encouragement from the United States to compete politically with the Communists. Yet no sooner was a peace treaty between the United States and Bulgaria ratified in June 1947 than Petkov was arrested on the floor of the Bulgarian parliament. He was tried, convicted, and hanged in September. There would be no further serious resistance to communism in Bulgaria for the next four decades.

In his book *Eastern Europe in the Postwar World,* author Thomas Simons refers to postwar Bulgaria as "a land of small farms and fanatical Communists." There are reasons that explain this fanaticism.

Historically, the Bulgarians looked on Russia and the Soviet Union as a friend and liberator, a view other countries did not share. "Not all that many years have passed since the battlefields of Bulgaria were littered with the bones of Russian warriors who died winning Bulgaria's independence from the Turks," wrote Soviet premier Nikita Khrushchev in his 1970 autobiography.

Besides this, Soviet domination and the stability it brought did not seem so terrible, even to a freedom-loving citizenry. War had been their constant companion for decades. When not at war with their neighbors over territory, the Bulgarians were at war with themselves—nationalist against liberal, communist against democrat. If nothing else, the Soviets provided stability and security for a populace that had known little of either. They built factories and industrial works in the newly expanding cities that gave jobs to a new class of urban immigrants who no longer had to scratch a meager living from the soil on small farms. Those Bulgarians who stayed in the rural areas now worked on large cooperative farms that used modern machinery, which greatly increased productivity. Both workers and farmers achieved a higher standard of living than they had ever known before.

For all these reasons, Bulgaria soon became Russia's most loyal satellite in the Communist bloc. There would be no Hungarian uprising, no Prague Spring, no Polish Solidarity movement in Bulgaria to challenge Soviet authority as in these other Eastern European countries. Dissent and demonstrations would be all but nonexistent there. Whatever

Georgi Dimitrov (left), Bulgaria's first Communist leader, looks admiringly at the man who trained him for the job, Soviet dictator Joseph Stalin, in a 1934 drawing. (Courtesy Library of Congress)

frustrations and dissatisfactions Bulgarians had with the strict regime they lived under, they kept them largely to themselves. For 40 years, Moscow would not have to worry about its "little brother," Bulgaria. It has no stauncher ally in the world.

In 1949 Premier Dimitrov died in Moscow while undergoing medical treatment and was soon replaced by Vulko Chervenkov (VUL-ko cher-VEN-kof) (1900–80), another protégé of Soviet leader Joseph Stalin. Chervenkov's enthusiasm for Soviet communism and his ruthlessness in crushing its enemies knew no bounds. While Dimitrov had destroyed the party's opponents, Chervenkov went about removing all those within the party itself who were a threat to his power. He sent thousands of loyal party members to their deaths following show trials, patterned after the ones that Stalin had conducted in Moscow in the 1930s. Chervenkov effectively ended all relations with the West and created a personality cult around himself that earned him the nickname "Little Stalin."

The Rise of Zhivkov

In 1953 Stalin died and Chervenkov suddenly found his position less secure. The following year at the sixth Party Congress, Todor Zhivkov (TO-dor JIV-kof) (see boxed biography), a long-time party official and World War II partisan leader, was named first secretary of the party's Central Committee. He became the youngest person in the Communist bloc to be so honored. Chervenkov hung on to power for two more years, but in 1956 the rise of Soviet leader Nikita Khrushchev and the rapid progress of de-Stalinization all but assured his downfall. At the April meeting of the Central Committee, Zhivkov publicly attacked Chervenkov and his personality cult and the leader was quickly replaced as premier by Anton Yugov (an-TON YOO-gof) (b. 1904).

Zhivkov's consolidation of power was completed when Khrushchev visited Bulgaria in 1962 and gave the younger man his blessing. That same year Chervenkov was expelled from the party, and Zhivkov ousted Yugov and made himself premier.

The new Communist leader was as much a pawn of the Soviets as his predecessor had been. He followed Soviet policy slavishly, ordered the Soviet flag flown alongside the Bulgarian flag, and declared the anniversary of the Russian Revolution a national holiday. On the other hand, Zhivkov appeared to be modest about his accomplishments, took pride in his ordinariness, and fully played the role of a man of the people. As the years passed, Zhivkov initiated modest economic reforms, liberalized censorship, and gradually opened the door to diplomatic relations and trade with the West.

But he was far from universally loved at home. In 1965, a year after Khrushchev's fall from power, Zhivkov's political enemies attempted a coup, the first such to occur in a Communist-bloc country. The coup failed and Zhivkov was quick to blame it on pro-Chinese elements.* More perceptive observers blamed the coup on Zhivkov himself and his rigid adherence to Soviet policy.

When the Soviets cracked down on Czechoslovakia's liberal movement in 1968, named Prague Spring, Zhivkov was quick to send troops to help the Soviets subdue the Czechs, while tightening censorship at home. Georgi Markov (ge-OR-gi MAR-kof) (1929–78), a leading

---

*The Chinese Communists had broken relations with the Soviets several years earlier.

Bulgarian writer, observed the contradictory nature of Zhivkov's char-acter on a drive he and other Bulgarian writers took with their leader in October 1964:

> . . . the natural question which occurred to me while the car was climbing the mountain road was: which one is the real Zhivkov? This rather courteous, agreeable interlocutor, who listened to us with inter-est, or the other one, who unceremoniously took it upon himself to decide the fate of the whole intelligentsia and dared decree what was true art and what was not with roughly the aesthetic equipment of a former sergeant-major.

Markov eventually became Zhivkov's protégé, but the corruption of the Communist regime finally drove him to defect to England in 1969. Markov proceeded to expose Zhivkov and his repressive government in writings he broadcast over Radio Free Europe. An enraged Zhivkov warned Markov to stop or he would be killed. But Markov continued his attacks on the Bulgarian Communists. On September 7, 1978, the exiled writer was crossing London's Waterloo Bridge when a tiny poisoned pel-let from the umbrella of an assassin entered his body. He died several days later. Zhivkov had made good on his threat.

In 1971 Zhivkov put forth a new national constitution that solidified the power of the Communist Party while appearing to give the people more freedom. With the aborted coup behind him and secure in his power, Zhivkov felt confident enough to strike a more statesmanlike pose on the world stage. He established diplomatic relations with West Ger-many and the United States, visited French president Charles de Gaulle (1890–1970), and improved relations with the Catholic Church in a visit with Pope Paul VI (1897–1978).

To prove he was a true Bulgarian, despite his close ties to Russia, Zhivkov championed his country's cultural heritage. He appointed his daughter Luidmilla head of the state commission on art and culture in 1973. Her efforts in this area reached its culmination in Bulgaria's 1,300th anniversary as a nation in 1981 with a national celebration of the arts. As part of the celebration, Zhivkov gave recognition to the Bulgar-ian Orthodox Church as a codefender of the nation and lifted some restrictions on public worship.

A Tarnished Reputation

But 1981 was also the year that Bulgaria's international reputation was seriously tarnished. Pope John Paul II (b. 1920) was wounded in an

TODOR ZHIVKOV (1911–1998)

He was the longest-ruling dictator in the Communist world and his very mediocrity may have been the secret of his success. "The Russians were perfectly satisfied to see their most secure Balkan fortress in the hand of an average man who was fully dependent on their will," wrote historian Nissen Oren. But for all his dependence on the Soviets, Zhivkov managed to do enough good for his country to make him as popular at home for many years as he was in Moscow.

He was born into a family of poor but devout peasants in a village outside of Sofia on September 7, 1911. After completing secondary school in the capital, Zhivkov became a printer in the state printing office, a trade he worked at for the next 12 years. He became involved in the local Communist party and became a full party member in 1932. Little is known of his political activities during the next decade, but he resurfaced as a partisan fighter against the occupying Germans in World War II. When the war ended, Zhivkov was elected to the new National Assembly as a Communist in 1945.

A loyal, if not brilliant, party man and Stalinist, Zhivkov rose through the ranks, becoming a full member of the Politburo, the small, controlling body of the national Communist Party, in 1951. Stalin's death two years later was a watershed in Bulgaria and other satellite countries. With the end of Stalinism, "homebred" Communists such as Zhivkov were favored over Moscow-trained leaders like Vulko Chervenkov. The rise of Nikita Khrushchev to power in the Soviet Union secured Zhivkov's position in Bulgaria, as the two were good friends.

Less formal than Chervenkov, Zhivkov presented himself as a "man of the people" whose humble beginnings and lack of charisma reinforced this public image. His strong allegiance to the Soviets was seen by many Bulgarians as fitting in a country where the Russians were still looked up to as liberators.

Among Zhivkov's achievements in his 33-year reign were the collectivization of Bulgarian agriculture, so complete it served as a model for other Eastern European countries; the resumption of relations with the West, however tentative; and a rapprochement with religion, cul-

assassination attempt by a Turkish nationalist who claimed the plot had been engineered by Bulgarian and Soviet intelligence agents. Although three Bulgarians accused as coconspirators were acquitted in 1986, Bulgaria's name was added to a U.S. State Department list of

minating in a visit with Pope Paul VI in 1975. On the negative side, his organized persecution of ethnic Turks in the 1980s was a dark stain on Bulgaria's international reputation. It only further discredited a government suspect for shady dealings with terrorists in the developing nations of the world.

With Communist governments collapsing all around him and a failing economy at home, Zhivkov became the scapegoat of his own party in 1989. He was deposed and put on trial for crimes against the Bulgarian people. Political crimes were difficult to pin on him because of a lack of evidence. But after a trial that lasted 18 months, Zhivkov was convicted of embezzlement of state funds and sentenced to a seven-year prison term. Due to heart problems, he was allowed to serve his time under house arrest. In February 1996 Zhivkov was acquitted of the original charges. He died unrepentant on August 5, 1998, at the age of 86. A dinosaur of the Communist world, Zhivkov had the misfortune to outlive all his patrons and protectors.

The longest-ruling dictator in the Communist world, Todor Zhivkov (left), is greeted by Polish prime minister Józef Cyrankiewicz (right) and first secretary of the Polish communist party, Władysław Gomułka, at the Warsaw airport in 1965. (Courtesy Library of Congress)

sponsors of terrorism. The United States had other reasons to suspect Bulgaria of assisting terrorists. Bulgaria did little to hide the fact that throughout the 1980s, it was supplying arms and military equipment to 36 nations around the world, many of them developing nations with active terrorist organizations.

Then in 1984 Zhivkov began what would be the most damaging campaign of his long regime. Fearing that the high birthrate of Bulgaria's ethnic Turkish population would turn Bulgarians into a minority within their own country, he initiated a drastic policy of forced assimilation. Turks who had been living peacefully in Bulgaria for centuries were told they would have to take Bulgarian names and could not speak Turkish in public. Rather than give up their ethnic identity, many Turks emigrated and returned to Turkey. Hundreds of others were forcibly expelled from Bulgaria, arrested and imprisoned, or even killed by Zhivkov's secret police. A total of more than 300,000 Turks left the country and returned to Turkey, creating one of the most massive exoduses in Balkan history. Whole communities in Bulgaria lost valuable workers in factories and businesses, while Turkey could not assimilate so many new immigrants and unemployment rates soared. Zhivkov later retracted his policy and many of the Turk nationals returned, but the damage had been done.

In 1982 Khrushchev's successor, Leonid Brezhnev (1906–82) died, and Zhivkov found himself without a patron. Yuri Andropov (1914–84), who replaced Brezhnev, disliked the Bulgarian leader because Zhivkov had not supported him for the position of party leader. Then in 1985 Mikhail Gorbachev (b. 1931) took the reins of power in Moscow. Gorbachev was a new kind of Soviet leader—pragmatic, energetic, and anxious to reform the Communist system in order to save it from itself. He made it clear to Bulgaria that it would have to reform itself as well if it wanted the continued support of its big brother. For Todor Zhivkov, the man who had followed the Soviet hard line through good times and bad, this was not encouraging news.

NOTES

p. 16 ". . . we were ordered to pack . . ." Michael Bar-Zohar, *Beyond Hitler's Grasp: The Heroic Rescue of Bulgaria's Jews* (Holbrook, Mass.: Adams Media Corporation, 1998), p. ix.

p. 18 "'a land of small farms . . .'" Thomas W. Simons, Jr., *Eastern Europe in the Post-war World*. (New York: St. Martin's Press, 1991), p. 59.

p. 18 "'Not all that many years . . .'" Nikita S. Khrushchev, *Khrushchev Remembers* (Boston: Little, Brown, 1970), p. 366.

p. 21 ". . . the natural question which occurred . . ." Georgi Markov, *The Truth That Killed* (New York: Ticknor & Fields, 1984), pp. 219–220.

p. 22 "'The Russians were perfectly satisfied . . .'" *Current Biography Yearbook 1976* (New York: H. W. Wilson Co., 1977), p. 460.

3

THE DEEPENING QUAGMIRE (1989 TO PRESENT)

Interestingly, the mass demonstration that rocked the seemingly unshakable Communist government of Bulgaria was not set off by economics or politics but environmental issues. In one sense, it was fitting. In 40 years, the Communist regime had transformed the natural beauty of Bulgaria into an environmental nightmare with recklessly unregulated industry and rampant pollution.

In October 1989 an international conference on the environment convened in Sofia. The choice of site must have held rich irony for local environmentalists since Sofia, and the surrounding area, was and remains today one of the most polluted regions in the country. Seizing the opportunity to make the world aware of the corrupt regime that could allow this to happen, the few dissident groups in Bulgaria organized a mass rally in the capital.

Five thousand Bulgarians marched on the National Assembly building on November 3 in what was the largest unofficial demonstration in the country in more than four decades. While the environment drove some to demonstrate, many more people used the issue as a starting place to protest against a government that had polluted nearly every aspect of Bulgarian life—economic, political, and social.

ZHELYU ZHELEV (b. 1935)

A good-natured man with good intentions is how one member of the National Assembly describes former president Zhelyu Zhelev. His good nature did not stop him from challenging the Communist government when it took real courage to do so. But his good intentions did not make him the most effective leader of his nation in his six years in office.

Zhelev studied philosophy at Sofia University in the 1960s. A brilliant student and independent thinker, he dared to criticize the father of Soviet socialism, Vladimir Lenin, in his doctoral dissertation. Although he got his degree, he was expelled from the Communist Party and was exiled to northern Bulgaria, where he lived with his family.

Zhelev soon became his country's most outspoken dissident. In his book *Fascism* he compared communism to the dictatorial governments of such fascist countries as Nazi Germany. The book was quickly banned in Bulgaria but became an underground best-seller and has since been translated into English.

Zhelev's uncompromising stand against the Communists made him the undisputed leader of the small Bulgarian dissident movement in the 1980s. He led the Union of Democratic Forces in its struggle against the state and was almost unanimously chosen to replace Petar Mladenov as president by the new National Assembly in 1990.

His popularity, however, gradually fell as one government after another came and went. Zhelev seemed to coexist too well with the former Communists. While he was never accused of political corruption, he was not perceived as taking a strong enough stand against it. His popularity with the Socialists may have sullied his reputation with many Bulgarians.

When he did take action, it often had mixed results. For example, when Zhelev refused to let the Socialists form a new government after the resignation of Zhan Videnov (jan VI-de-nof), he made a strong

The protestors had chosen their moment wisely. To suppress the demonstration with so many foreigners present for the conference would have been an embarrassment for the government, and it allowed the protest to run its course.

statement against the Socialists. But he also left his country to flounder without any government at all.

"The fall of the Socialist Party from power is inevitable, as it has proved unable to lead the country out of the crisis," Zhelev said back in May 1996. Unable himself to lead his country, his own fall from power may also have been inevitable, and he was not chosen as a candidate in 1996. A private citizen once more, Zhelev is a leading spokesperson for a better, more democratic Bulgaria.

"There are a lot of people who are dissatisfied," he said in a 2001 interview. They are struggling with unemployment, poverty, economic hardship, which are the traits of Bulgaria's transition from Communism to democracy."

A courageous dissident for decades, Zhelyu Zhelev disappointed many of his supporters in his six-year tenure as president by getting along too well with the former Communists. (AP Photo/Aris Saris)

The Fall of Zhivkov

The demonstration sent shock waves through the Communist government, whose leaders had until then felt confident they could avert the fate of similar regimes throughout Eastern Europe. Anxious to nip any discontent in the bud, the younger, moderate wing of the party, led by Foreign Minister Petar Mladenov (PE-tar me-LA-de-nof) (1936–2000), offered the people a scapegoat. Todor Zhivkov, who had ruled Bulgaria for 33 years, was 78 years old, weak, and out of touch with the country he had governed so long. Many people blamed Zhivkov for a depressed economy and such unpopular policies as the anti-Turk campaign in the 1980s. Mladenov and his colleagues in the party hierarchy forced Zhivkov to resign. The announcement was made on November 10, 1989, only a week after the historic demonstration in Sofia.

With Zhivkov's fall, wrote Clyde Haberman in the *New York Times*, Bulgaria was no longer "in the rear guard of the Communist world, plodding along amid the rush of events. . . . A new breed of Bulgarian dissidents has begun to speak out to a degree rarely heard in this Slavic nation."

With Mladenov as president, the Communists cleaned house, removing hard-liners from high positions in the party and replacing them with

The jubilation of these demonstrators at a November 1989 rally in Sofia at the resignation of Zhivkov would not last long. His replacement, Petar Mladenov, whose picture is held by the woman, would continue Communist policies, until he was forced to resign less than a year later. (AP Photo/Dusan Vranic)

moderates. At the same time, a group of 16 pro-democratic parties formed a coalition and called themselves the Union of Democratic Forces (UDF). The leader of the UDF was a former Communist and one of Bulgaria's few well-known dissidents, Zhelyu Zhelev (JE-yoo JE-lef) (see boxed biography). Zhelev, a philosopher and writer, had been expelled from the party in 1965 when he openly questioned some of the theories of Soviet leader Vladimir Lenin (1870–1924).

In January 1990 the Communists agreed to meet for talks with the UDF, while Zhivkov, the longest-ruling leader in the Communist world, was arrested and charged with numerous crimes against the Bulgarian people. He later became the first Communist leader to be sentenced in a court of law. By putting all the blame for Bulgaria's problems on Zhivkov, the Communists hoped to stay in power. But under increasing pressure from the people and UDF leaders, they agreed to the first free and open elections in more than 40 years of Communist rule.

From Communist to Socialist

The government, however, was not in retreat; it was merely regrouping. In a clever move, the Bulgarian Communist Party changed its name to the less offensive Bulgarian Socialist Party (BSP) and prepared for the June elections of delegates to the National Assembly. Although unpopular, the Socialists were still better organized and better known than their new and inexperienced opponents. As a result, they received 48 percent of all votes cast and won a majority of seats in the new assembly.

But the struggle was far from over. That summer anti-Communist students, intellectuals, and other dissidents set up tents in central Sofia in what they declared to be a "Communist-free zone." Others referred to it as the "City of Truth."

Petar Mladenov, Zhivkov's successor, was shown on a videotape made in December 1989 during demonstrations saying: "The best thing to do is to bring in the tanks." A remark that a few years before would have had no impact was now inflammatory. Thousands cried out for Mladenov to resign as party general-secretary and president. He did and was replaced by an overwhelming vote in the assembly by Dr. Zhelev, who became the first non-Communist president of Bulgaria since World War

II. The presidency, however, was largely a ceremonial office with little real authority.

The Socialists clung stubbornly to power, but their grip was slipping. With democratic governments coming to power in country after country in Eastern Europe, the Bulgarian regime became more and more isolated. A general strike that largely paralyzed the nation rendered the government all but helpless and unable to govern. The Socialist government resigned before the end of 1990.

The Failure of Democracy

A coalition government took over, largely led by the UDF, whose members held key positions in the cabinet. The new Republic of Bulgaria (previously the Communist-led People's Republic) adapted a Western-style democratic constitution and scheduled new parliamentary elections for October 1991. This time, the UDF was the undisputed winner, with the Socialists running second. Just behind them was the ethnic Turkish party, the Movement for Rights and Freedoms (MRF), which united with UDF in a new coalition that formed a government in November. This government, led by Prime Minister Filip Dimitrov (FI-lip di-mi-TROF) (b. 1955), promised full rights to citizens, a better life under a free market economy, and other reforms, but few of its promises were fulfilled. The Socialists were still a considerable force in the assembly, and the machinery of the old Communist Party was still in place. To dismantle the state would be a major undertaking, and the democratic government had neither the strength nor the support to accomplish this feat.

Within a year, the people's optimism had turned to skepticism. The UDF had lost the support of the MRF, and a number of its own supporters had joined the dissenters. Its stringent economic policies had turned the trade unions, private businesses, and even the Bulgarian Orthodox Church against it. At the end of 1992 the government resigned after a no-confidence vote from the National Assembly.

Another coalition, anti-Communist government was formed under Lyuben Berov (LYOO-ben BE-rof) (b. 1925), an economics professor. Berov vowed to take industry and big business out of the state's grip by allowing private individuals and companies to run it. But the financial mess he inherited from the Dimitrov regime made the task all but impossible. Berov tried to balance the budget by making deep cuts in health, education, and national defense, which brought sharp criticism from many people. Angry farmers, incensed by the slow pace of returning collective farms to individual farmers, came to the capital to demonstrate in April 1993.

Besieged from every side, Berov stepped down in September 1994, and President Zhelev appointed a caretaker government to prepare the way for new elections.

What economic reforms Berov had delivered had not been well received by the people. Their everyday lives seemed to get worse, not better. The torturous process of transition from the state-run economy to a free market made many Bulgarians long for the stability of the former Communist state. In fall 1994 the people voted to return the Bulgarian Socialist Party to power.

A Corrupt Government

The same movement back to former Communist leaders had taken place in Poland, Hungary, and Romania. The difference was that in these countries, the former Communists were careful to continue democratic policies, albeit more cautiously. In Bulgaria, the Socialists had no intention of dismantling the state they had spent 40 years building.

Zhan Videnov (b. 1959), became the new prime minister. A 35-year-old Moscow-trained Communist, Videnov was probably the most dedicated leftist governing in the region. But at first, Western observers viewed him and his new breed of communism as a breath of fresh air. "They saw the Videnov technocrats come in, wearing nice suits and speaking English, and said these people will move Bulgaria ahead," said political analyst Evgenii Dainov (ef-GE-ni DAI-nof). "They did nothing of the kind."

Under Videnov, Bulgaria took three steps back from democratic reform. No further movement was made toward privatization of state industry, even after the World Bank offered funds, support, and retraining for workers to help ease the transition from a state economy to a free market. Western investments were discouraged, and several of the biggest foreign investors left the country. Much worse, thousands of young Bulgarians were leaving their homeland to look for better job opportunities abroad.

Videnov's government had the dubious distinction of being the only post-Communist government in Eastern Europe to show no interest in joining the North Atlantic Treaty Organization (NATO), an international group of 15 Western nations formed in 1949 to defend themselves collectively against aggression. As one foreign diplomat put it: "Bulgaria will not do anything with regards to NATO which it is not totally confident that the Russians approve of and want to happen." The Socialist government renewed friendly relations with Russia, which promised increased trade and other useful exchanges in return for a renewal of the close ties the two countries enjoyed in the Soviet era.

But national self-interest and ideology were not the only motives for the government's hard-line policies. There was also personal greed. Instead of privatizing state-owned industry, government officials allowed party members in business to help themselves to literally billions in assets in floundering companies. Then they allowed them to send the money abroad to be stashed away in foreign banks. Within a short time nearly all of Bulgaria's 47 state-owned and private banks were insolvent. The entire country was going bankrupt while a few people were growing rich on the misery of the masses. "People's savings were going into a black hole," observed one Western banker. Thousands lined up at banks to remove their savings before it was too late. "I haven't seen a time like this since after the war, when my father had to sell his shoes for bread," complained one elderly woman waiting to withdraw her life's savings. "When I get my money, I'm keeping it at home. I have no confidence in any bank anymore."

Inflation soared, as did the prices of staples like bread. Sofia and other cities were filled with long lines of people waiting to buy a loaf of bread that they could barely afford. Workers' salaries by early 1996 had hit rock bottom—$30 a month, lower than Albania, the poorest country in Europe.

Even law and order, one area that the Communists had prided themselves on, was unraveling. Crime and violence were becoming rampant. The crisis reached a peak on October 2, 1996, when former prime minister Andrei Lukanov (an-DREI loo-KA-nof) (1939–96), who had led two previous Socialist governments in 1989 and 1990, was gunned down in broad daylight by an assassin as he was leaving his home. Rumors spread quickly that Lukanov, who was one of Videnov's sharpest critics, was killed for political reasons. In November 2003 construction magnate Angel Vasilev and four others were convicted of Lukanov's death and sentenced to life in prison.

A New President

Betrayed by the Socialists, whom they had trusted to make life better in a world of chaos and change, the Bulgarian people took their anger to the polls. In late October 1996 the first round of elections for president were held. President Zhelev, who had lost much of his popularity by railing against the Socialist government but doing little to improve the situation, lost his bid for reelection in the primary. Ivan Marazov (i-VAN ma-RA-zof), the Socialist candidate, came in a poor second to UDF candidate Petar Stoyanov (PE-tar sto-YA-nof) (b. 1952), who won about 45 percent of the vote. A month later Stoyanov won the final round with more than 60 percent of the vote.

Numerous strikes and demonstrations took place across the country as the people voiced their deep displeasure with the Socialist government. Losing all ability to govern under the pressure of civil unrest, Prime Minister Videnov finally resigned in late December 1996. Interior Minister Nikolai Dobrev (ni-KO-la DO-bref) was nominated to replace him, but President Zhelev, still in office, refused to allow Dobrev to form a new government.

Bulgaria, already in dire economic straits, entered the new year without a stable government. Basic services were now endangered. Hospitals closed in some cities, and in others the doctors, shamefully underpaid, sent home all but the sickest of their patients. Schools, unable to afford to heat classrooms, reduced class periods and sent students home early. Unable to pay for fuel to keep their homes warm, families and many older people scoured the nearest forest for wood to burn. The country was falling apart.

The seething rage of the people boiled over. Tens of thousands took to the streets to protest. On January 10, 1997, they broke into the National Assembly building and went on a rampage. They smashed furniture,

Frustration and joy are mingled in the faces of these demonstrators at an opposition rally in Sofia on January 13, 1997. Only six days later a new democratically elected president, Petar Stoyanov, would take office and the besieged Socialists would be out of power by May. (AP Photo/Dimitar Deinov)

destroyed computers, and set fire to an office. For 10 hours they block-aded the entrance and prevented a hundred legislators from leaving the assembly building. The police were called in and with clubs and guns drawn, dispersed the crowd in a bloody melee that left both police and protesters injured. "This is the anger of people who had nothing to lose," said Yordan Sokolov (yor-DAN so-KO-lof), a leading spokesman for the UDF in the National Assembly.

Order was restored, but the protests continued. Day after day, the streets of Sofia were filled with demonstrators, disrupting traffic and car-rying protest signs.

The Socialists' term of office would not expire until 1998, but the peo-ple wanted them out much sooner, calling for new elections by May. The Socialists stubbornly refused to resign, promising only to enter into a "wider dialogue" with their political opponents. But a serious division was developing within the Socialist Party itself, with moderates calling for the hard-liners to initiate some reforms and move up the date for elections.

On January 19, 1997, Petar Stoyanov was installed as Bulgaria's second democratically elected president. Forty thousand people jammed into Sofia's streets to see the man on whom their frail hopes were now pinned. The 44-year-old lawyer and former soccer star spoke to them of a new tomorrow, of market reforms that would save the plummeting economy, and a new Bulgaria where young and old alike would find a better, brighter future. He also called for new national elections and punishment for corrupt politicians.

"In the last four years," Stoyanov said, addressing the crowd, "Bulgaria has seen only an imitation of reforms linked with corruption and arrogant disregard of public opinion. The future of the kids has always been the main concern of every Bulgarian. We have to offer them a society they wish to live in."

After 23 days of public protest, 25,000 students and other dissidents held the largest rally yet in the capital. It was followed by a general strike by the three largest trade unions. Realizing it had to compromise or face greater troubles, the government reluctantly agreed to move up elections to the fall of 1997.

This was not good enough for the Bulgarian people. As protests grew more massive, a transportation strike paralyzed the country. On February 4, President Stoyanov called for an emergency meeting with government leaders. After four hours of intense negotiations, he emerged to announce that the Socialists were stepping down from power and had agreed to hold general elections no later than April 20. The crowd cheered and lifted Stoyanov on their shoulders, carrying him through streets filled with dancing, joyful people.

Stoyanov immediately appointed a caretaker government led by Sofia mayor Stefan Sofiyanski until the elections could be held. When elections were held in April, the UDF won big—137 out of 240 assembly seats. The Socialists took only 58 seats. A new coalition government was formed under the leadership of 48-year-old economist Ivan Kostov, who was elected prime minister.

In its first session, held on May 7, 1997, the new assembly pledged to the Bulgarian people that they would work to improve the economy, reduce crime, and bring Bulgaria closer to the European mainstream. But all the government's good intentions brought little relief to the Bulgarian people. Through the year 1998 not a single important privatization

A former soccer star, Petar Stoyanov (right) was Bulgaria's second democratically elected president. (Courtesy NATO)

transaction took place. By 1999, only a little more than 30 percent of all assets in the economy were in private hands, including just one bank. This fell far short of the goal set by the International Monetary Fund (IMF) to have all banks in private hands by 1999.

At the end of June 1999, Finance Minister Mouravei Radev made the bold announcement that 40 percent of state assets were to be sold and numerous state-owned companies shut down. The government got a much-needed boost in November when U.S. president Bill Clinton (b. 1946) became the first American head of state to visit Bulgaria. In his meetings with President Stoyanov, Clinton vowed to increase U.S. aid to the country if the economy stabilized and the movement toward a democratic system continued. A month later the European Union (EU), a trading bloc of mostly Western European nations, formally invited Bulgaria and six other countries to join its ranks.

A Monarch Returns to Power

In April 2001 ex-king Simeon II (see sidebar, chapter 4) arrived in his homeland to take up permanent residence. Within days, Simeon announced plans to form a new political group, the National Movement Simeon II (NMSII).

The former king's entrance into the political arena was not a complete surprise. Since his first visit to Bulgaria in 1996 after nearly 50 years in exile, he had been urged by many Bulgarians to take a leadership position—either as a restored monarch or as a candidate for president or prime minister. Since then, increased dissatisfaction with politicians on both the right and left made Simeon, a nonpolitical unifier from a fondly remembered past, a more attractive alternative. While some accused Simeon of wanting to restore the monarchy, many more were impressed by his stated desire to help restore confidence in government "without," as he said, "a big philosophical discussion on monarchy and republic at this stage."

In the parliamentary election of June 2001, the NMSII swept to victory with 43 percent of the vote, more than the combined votes cast for the UDF and the BSP. One seat short of a majority, the NMSII formed a coalition with the fourth largest political party, the MRF, and formed a new government with Simeon as prime minister. He became the first former monarch to become a political leader in post-Communist Eastern Europe.

Espousing a centralist stance, Simeon's government was bold in its promises to the nation. The new prime minister vowed to end unemployment and poverty, expand economic growth, and improve the living standard within 800 days of taking power. It was a message that many Bulgarians were eager to hear. "He is Bulgaria's last chance to get out of the morass of poverty and corruption," said Alexander Shavchev, an out-of-work engineer. "This country deserves a politician of a real Western brand at last."

A Familiar Pattern

The Bulgarian people were impatient for change. After only 100 days in power, the Simeon government was confronted by thousands of protestors who saw little improvement in their lives since his takeover. In the presidential election of December 2001, they expressed their dissatisfaction at the ballot box, electing Socialist Party leader Georgi Purvanov (b. 1957) president over the incumbent Petar Stoyanov, 54 percent to 46 percent. The election had the lowest turnout of any election since communism's fall, signaling a growing apathy among voters. "I'm not going to vote anymore," retiree Yona Dimitrova told one reporter, "because politicians are all the same—they don't give a damn about ordinary people."

By late 2002, after 18 months in power, Simeon's popularity dropped from 70 percent to 25 percent. "I respect the people too much to promise things without knowing that I can deliver," said a sadder but wiser Simeon. But there have been signs of improvement. There was a 4 percent economic growth in Bulgaria from 2000 to 2002. Both Simeon and President Purvanov have made meaningful efforts to gain their country's membership in the EU and NATO by 2004. Disillusioned yet hopeful, the Bulgarian people soldier on, looking to a brighter day.

NOTES

p. 28 "A good-natured man . . ." *New York Times*, January 15, 1997, p. A3.

p. 29 "'The fall of the Socialist Party . . .'" Veselin Zhelev, "Bulgarians Line Up for Fuel," The Associated Press News Service, May 27, 1996. CD NewsBank.

p. 29 "'There are a lot of people . . .'" *New York Times*, December 11, 2001, p. A4.

p. 30 "in the rear guard of the Communist world . . ." Bernard Gwertzman and Michael T. Kauffman, eds., *The Collapse of Communism* (New York: Times Books, 1990), p. 186.

p. 31 "'The best thing to do . . .'" James Naughton, *Traveller's Literary Companion: Eastern & Central Europe* (Lincolnwood, Ill.: Passport Books, 1996), p. 289.

p. 33 "'They saw the Videnov technocrats come in . . .'" Christine Spolar, "Bulgaria Pays Price for Lagging on Market Reforms," *Washington Post*, July 7, 1996, p. A21. CD NewsBank.

p. 34 "'Bulgaria will not do anything . . .'" *New York Times*, April 28, 1995, p. A11.

p. 34 "'People's savings were going . . .'" *New York Times*, October 28, 1996, p. A6.

p. 34 "'I haven't seen a time like this . . .'" *Washington Post*, July 7, 1996, p. A21.

p. 36 "'This is the anger . . .'" *Connecticut Post*, January 11, 1997, p. A5.

p. 37 "'In the last four years . . .'" Veselin Toshkov, "Bulgaria's President Sworn In," Associated Press News Service, January 19, 1997. CD NewsBank.

p. 39 "'Without a big philosophical discussion . . .'" *New York Times*, June 17, 2001, p. 3.

p. 39 "'He is Bulgaria's last chance . . .'" *Connecticut Post*, July 13, 2001, p. A16.

p. 40 "'I'm not going to vote anymore . . .'" *New York Times*, December 13, 2002, p. A14.

p. 40 "'I respect the people . . .'" *New York Times*, see above.

PART II
Bulgaria Today

4

GOVERNMENT

At the end of 2003, the government of the Republic of Bulgaria seemed no better off than it had been since independence. Both democratic and Socialist administrations had failed in their attempts to build a healthy new nation on the crumbling foundation of the old one. Yet the structure of government set up by the revised constitution of 1991 is a strong one. It only needs skilled politicians who are willing to work unselfishly and courageously for the public good to implement it.

The Three Branches of National Government

Many of the political institutions existing in Bulgaria today were conceived under communism, but they had little if any power then to act independently. The National Assembly, the legislative body, was a mere rubber stamp for the reigning Communist Party's politburo. The courts were another arm of the state with little independence.

Much of this changed with the collapse of communism and the rise of the first freely elected government in 1990. A new constitution adopted at Veliko Turnovo (ve-LI-ko TUR-no-vo) in July 1991 turned the National Assembly into a truly representative legislative body of 240 members, directly elected by proportional representation. If the National Assembly has been perceived as weak in recent years, it is not because it is powerless. A political stalemate has often resulted from the conflicting interests of representatives of the BSP, the UDF, and the NMSII.

The Republic of Bulgaria has chosen, as have so many of the newly independent Eastern Bloc countries, a parliamentary form of government. The president, while officially the head of state, has far less power than the prime minister, the political leader of the party in power. The president is, however, commander in chief of the armed forces, serves as his country's representative abroad, and chooses the prime minister with the approval of the National Assembly. He can, as former president Zhelev has done, refuse to name a new prime minister and create a caretaker government while calling for new elections.

The prime minister, with his cabinet of 17 ministers, called the Council of Ministers, runs the government. Each minister is responsible for one facet of government, from finance and foreign affairs to education and the environment.

GEORGI PURVANOV (b. 1957)

Bulgaria's third president since independence is the first former Communist to win that office. Georgi Purvanov was born on June 28, 1957, and graduated from Sofia University St. Kliment Orhidski in 1981. The same year, he joined the Bulgarian Communist Party (BCP).

For the next decade Purvanov worked as a historical researcher, earning a master's and a doctoral degree in history from Sofia University. In 1990 the Communist Party changed its name to the Bulgarian Socialist Party (BSP). Purvanov was elected a member of the BSP's Supreme Council in December 1991. He served as deputy chairman of the Supreme Council from 1994 to 1996, at which time he was elected chairman.

When the government of Zhan Videnov crumbled under national protests in 1997, Purvanov turned down a mandate to form a new government in order to help end a growing crisis. For his self-sacrificing actions, Purvanov won the admiration of many Bulgarians. He worked hard to turn the BSP from a tradition-bound Soviet-like organization into a modern, European-style social-democratic party. Although anxious to revive relations with Russia, he has also been a strong advocate for his country to join both NATO and the EU.

When sworn in as president on January 19, 2002, Purvanov promised to represent all Bulgarians, regardless of their politics. A strong nationalist and dedicated reformer, Purvanov may be just the kind of president Bulgaria needs in this difficult time of transition.

Bulgarian president Georgi Purvanov has worked hard to build the Bulgarian Socialist Party into a modern European-style political party. (Courtesy NATO)

The president is elected directly by the people and can serve no more than two five-year terms. The prime minister and his party govern until a crisis leads to a vote of no confidence in the National Assembly, and then the government must step down, as the Socialists finally did in early 1997. Then new elections are scheduled to determine the next government. In January 2003 the UDF called for a no-confidence vote for the Simeon government. The motion was overturned. However, three deputy ministers were dismissed shortly after in a cabinet shakeup.

The judicial branch in many ways has undergone the least changes since 1991. The members of the Supreme Court, the highest judicial body in Bulgaria, are elected to five-year terms by the National Assembly. Reform barely touched the court, and judges, until recently, remained some of the poorest paid and least respected professionals in the country. In a 1991 poll, less than 2 percent of the Bulgarian people trusted in the fairness of the courts. More recent reforms have improved the judicial system, although most people retain their skepticism. There are 105 provincial courts and many more municipal courts that try minor offenses at the local level.

For decades, Bulgaria was politically divided into 28 districts. In 1987 the Communists consolidated these districts into nine provinces, known as *oblasti* (O-bla-sti) (singular *oblast*). The oblasti are governed locally by the People's Councils, whose members are elected for terms of 30 months. They attend to local services, such as police and road repairs.

SIMEON SAXE-COBURG GOTHA (b. 1937)

"I'll do what I can, but I do not have the vocation of a spare wheel," the ex-king of Bulgaria told an interviewer in early 1997, soon after his historic first visit to his homeland in nearly 50 years. "If things go fine without me, then this is a blessing for Bulgaria and for me."

But things did not go well for Bulgaria in the late 1990s under a corrupt Socialist regime, and a little more than five years after his interview, Simeon founded his own political party and won a parliamentary election. He was appointed prime minister of his country, the first royal to take charge as a political leader in post-Communist Eastern Europe.

Simeon's first reign in Bulgaria began at the tender age of six, following the mysterious death of his father, King Boris, in 1943. When the Communists took over the country three years later, they abolished the monarchy and Simeon was forced to flee with his mother, daughter of the king of Italy, to Egypt. Soon after, he settled in Spain, where he grew to adulthood, married a Spanish aristocrat, and became a successful business consultant.

In May 1996 the exiled king returned home at the invitation of Bulgarian intellectuals who hoped he would become a leader in post-Communist Bulgaria and help restore order to a troubled land. Simeon was greeted warmly on his arrival by half a million of his country's people.

When his new nationalist political movement was victorious in the parliamentary election of June 2001, Simeon made more promises to the people than he, or anyone else, could keep. Having been only slightly more effective at improving living conditions and the economy than the government he replaced, Simeon knows his days in power are numbered if he cannot produce results. He believes the country will improve before the next scheduled parliamentary election, in 2005. "I am firmly committed to doing a good job and showing the world that Bulgaria is a proper democracy," he said in a 2001 interview. Only time will tell if he can match his words with actions.

Political Parties

Until recently, the NMSII was the largest and most powerful political party in the country. By early 2003, however, they had dropped in popularity to third place, behind the Socialists and UDF. The BSP, in and out

Simeon II (right), former king and current leader of the new Nationalist Movement Party, was elected prime minister in 2001. (Courtesy NATO)

of power twice since independence, is poised to retake power again if the government of Prime Minister Simeon seriously falters.

The UDF has also regained strength at the NMSII's expense. A true coalition, it was originally made up of 10 organizations that had different beliefs but held several goals in common. They all wanted to see Bulgaria become a country with a constitutional government that provides its citizens with democratic freedoms and a free market economy. The coalition quickly expanded to include six more groups. Under the leadership of Zhelyu Zhelev, Bulgaria's most visible dissident, the UDF became an effective dissident party against the Communists after the fall of Zhivkov, and later an effective opposition party against the Socialists. There is a great diversity of interests and concerns within the coalition, including such narrowly focused groups as the ecologically minded Green Party. While dissension among the various groups weakened the party for years, it is stronger today than it has been for some time.

Among the smaller political parties in Bulgaria, the most interesting and visible is the Movement for Rights and Freedoms (MRF). It represents the rights of the Turkish minority in Bulgaria. In the face of deepening anti-Turkish feeling in Bulgaria, the party broadened its stand on civil rights in 1991. While denying any call for complete autonomy of Turks within Bulgaria, the MRF has taken a strong stand on the protection of the rights of Turks and other ethnic minorities. At present, two ministers in Simeon's cabinet are representatives of the MRF.

Foreign Relations

For four decades following World War II, Bulgaria's foreign policy was largely built on its close relationship with the Soviet Union. That policy continued with Russia after the collapse of communism, under the two governments of the BSP. Promises from the Russians of military and economic aid kept Bulgaria's Socialists firmly within the Russian sphere. Although Bulgaria has been a member of NATO's Partnership for Peace program since 1997, the Socialist government was hesitant to apply for full NATO membership for fear of offending the Russians. The Simeon centralist government has aggressively promoted NATO membership and closer ties with the United States and other Western nations.

In early September 2002 President Purvanov made his first trip to the United States since becoming president. He met with Secretary of State Colin Powell, who applauded Bulgaria's efforts as a member of the world antiterrorist coalition and its efforts toward political stability. He also warned that if Bulgaria were to gain NATO membership, it would not mean that the nation should relax its efforts in ending widespread political corruption, crime, and illegal trafficking in weapons. In May 2003 Bulgaria became a full member of NATO, along with Estonia, Latvia, Lithuania, Romania, Slovakia, and Slovenia.

On September 19, 2003, Bulgaria celebrated a centenary of the establishment of diplomatic relations with the United States. On hand in Sofia were six former U.S. ambassadors to Bulgaria. As the two countries enter a second century of relations, their ties appear to be growing stronger.

"I have spent almost all my life in the West; my democratic feelings are unquestionable," said Prime Minister Simeon in a 2001 interview. "I have looked at events in the region from a wide perspective."

That perspective will hopefully place Bulgaria in a far better position in the modern world than it has ever occupied before.

Armed Forces

Bulgaria has its own army, navy, and air and air-defense forces, as well as a small internal force and civil defense force. Its annual military expenditure is $356 million. As a new member of NATO, Bulgaria's military operations will continue to grow in the future with U.S. aid and expertise.

The United States sees Bulgaria as one of its best new friends in Europe. During the 1999 UN action against Bosnia, a former part of Yugoslavia, Bulgaria gave UN troops access to its airspace. It was one of only four UN Security Council members to support the U.S.-led war in Iraq in 2003. When the war formally ended, Bulgaria sent a security force of 500 troops to help keep peace in the troubled Middle Eastern country.

In 2003 U.S. military officials visited Bulgarian military installations to examine them as possible bases for American and NATO troops. The Bulgarian government is eager for an increased American presence in its country for reasons of national security and economic growth. The city of Plovdiv has been the site of a NATO training program since 1999. An airfield and an air base outside the city have been upgraded in anticipation of the arrival of more American troops.

"Bulgaria has not managed to get beyond the syndrome of needing a big brother," said Defense Minister Nikolay Svinarov. "But this time I believe decisions will be taken as partners, not alone in Moscow or Washington, D.C."

NOTES
p. 46 "'I'll do what I can . . .'" *New York Times*, January 31, 1997, p. A12.
p. 46 "'I am firmly committed . . .'" Central Europe Review. Available on-line. URL: www.ce-review.org/01/22/Kadiev22.html. Downloaded on October 15, 2003.
p. 48 "'I have spent almost all my life . . .'" Central Europe Review, same as above.
p. 49 "'Bulgaria has not managed . . .'" *Los Angeles Times*, May 28, 2003, p. A4.

5

RELIGION

In May 2002 Pope John Paul II visited Bulgaria, the first pope ever to do so. "I say to all that I have never ceased to love the Bulgarian people," the pope told the crowds of people who turned out to greet him on this historic occasion. His words ended any doubts that the alleged involvement of the Bulgarian secret service in the 1981 attempt on his life had been forgotten and forgiven. Bulgarian Orthodox religious leaders, however, were generally cool to the pope's visit, fearing it would lead to more Catholic converts and weaken their position. Secular leaders such as President Purvanov were eager to welcome the pope, whose visit could only improve Bulgaria's standing in Europe as it awaited accession to the EU. Religion, as it has for centuries, continues to play a central role in Bulgarian life.

The Bulgarian Orthodox Church— Past and Present

The Bulgars adopted Christianity in A.D. 864, becoming one of the first peoples of Eastern Europe to do so. The religious writing of Bulgarian monks and priests were crucial in converting other peoples in Eastern Europe, including the Russians. The Bulgarian Orthodox Church, one of the many orthodox communities in Eastern Europe, was, and remains, fiercely nationalistic.

Czar Simeon I established the Bulgarian Orthodox Church in the 900s. His palace library was a treasure house of religious learning, and he employed monks to copy precious church manuscripts for posterity. It is said Simeon himself put together a collection of sermons known as *slava* (SLA-va).

When the Bulgarian Empire was swallowed up by the Byzantines, religion again was in the forefront of the resistance. In the 10th century, a Bulgarian priest named Bogomil (BO-go-mil) began a religious movement. The Bogomils, as his disciples were called, were passionately nationalistic, opposed to Byzantine domination and culture, and viewed the material world as the work of the devil. So appealing were the sect's precepts that they soon spread over much of Southern and Eastern Europe, taking different names in each country. By the 15th century, Bogomilism was weakened and largely vanquished by the Bulgarian Orthodox Church and the Byzantine Empire, but Bogomilism's influence continued. "There is no doubt," wrote historian David Marshall Lang, "that [the Bogomils] helped to destroy Bulgarian national unity, and pave the way for ultimate Turkish conquest."

When the Communists took over Bulgaria after World War II, they recognized that the Bulgarian Orthodox Church was closely linked to Bulgarian nationalism and did everything they could to undermine its power and influence. Once a major landholder, the church was stripped of its property. The legendary Rila Monastery (see boxed feature), was turned into a national museum. While clergy were not banned from practicing, their appointment had to be approved by the state, which also paid their salaries. Church officials and clergymen who did not strictly adhere to the rules laid down by the government were dismissed, imprisoned, or sent into exile. The number of Orthodox priests shrunk from 3,312 in 1947, the year after the Communists came to power, to 1,700 in 1985.

When Todor Zhivkov fell from power in 1989 and the Communists began to lose their grip on the country, Bulgaria experienced a religious revival. Church holidays were reinstated. A flurry of baptisms and weddings filled church calendars. Christmas 1990 was a joyous national celebration. An Orthodox seminary in Sofia reopened its doors and took in more than 100 students. Rila and other monasteries were returned to a grateful church. Religious expression was something to be celebrated after the long, dark night of communism.

But the Bulgarian Orthodox Church today faces serious problems. Forty years of atheistic Communist rule has left its mark. While an estimated 84

The fall of communism brought a revival of the Bulgarian Orthodox Church. Here, a young girl in traditional folk dress kisses the hand of a beaming Maxim, head of the Orthodox Church, on Palm Sunday, 1997. (AP Photo/Dragan Filipovic)

percent of Bulgarians are Orthodox Church members, as many as 65 percent of them do not practice their faith today. There is also a severe shortage of priests, with many older priests facing retirement age. Younger liberal religious leaders are in conflict with their elders, who grew up under the Communist regime and have been accused of collaboration and corruption.

Hopefully, this new generation of religious leaders will bring a much needed moral strength and spiritual focus to a church that has too long stood more for nationalism and ritual ceremony than a deep and abiding faith.

Bulgarian Jews—A Proud Record

Bulgaria's Jews are mostly descended from Jewish exiles of Spain who fled that country in the 16th century to escape persecution. They settled in Bulgarian cities and were largely assimilated into the population.

Unlike Jews living in other European countries, Bulgaria's 50,000 Jews were spared the fate of the concentration camps and gas chambers of Nazi Germany, thanks to the compassion and determination of the Bulgarian

THE RILA MONASTERY

The more than 100 medieval monasteries of Bulgaria have been much more than homes for pious monks. For centuries they were centers of learning, repositories of great literature and art, and shining symbols of Slavic civilization when that civilization seemed in danger of disappearing.

The Monastery of St. John of Rila is the largest and most celebrated of the Bulgarian monasteries and is one of the oldest in all Europe. It lies 75 miles (121 km) south of Sofia in the Rila Mountains, a landscape of breathtaking beauty. The monastery was founded by the holy hermit Ivan Rilski (i-VAN RIL-ski) (ca. 876–946), who has since been canonized as Saint Ivan of Rila, the patron saint of Bulgaria.

A stronghold of Bulgarian culture through centuries of oppression under the Byzantines and the Turks, Rila Monastery has suffered every indignity. It has been robbed, burned, and turned into a museum by the Communists. Yet it has survived. Today it has been returned to the Bulgarian Orthodox Church and has been named one of the world's greatest cultural historical sites by the United Nations. In May 2002 Pope John Paul II toured the monastery during his first visit to Bulgaria.

Rila's painted icons, frescoes, and murals, depicting biblical scenes, still inspire awe hundreds of years after its gifted monks created them.

In his poem "Near the Rila Monastery," famed Bulgarian author Ivan Vazov (i-VAN VA-zof) (1850–1921) describes the beauty of the surrounding natural landscape. His words express what millions of Bulgarians feel about this national treasure:

> Now I am truly home—a world it is
> Which I adore and seek. Here I breathe freely
> And lighter feel; a deep tranquillity
> Now fills my breast and waves of new life, sweeping
> Into my soul, thrill me with new sensations,
> New strength, might and poetic revelations . . .

government and its people. Although an ally of Germany, Bulgaria dragged its feet on the deporting of Jews, knowing they were going to almost certain death. They eventually reversed the anti-Jewish laws the Nazis had foisted upon them early in the war. When the war ended in German defeat, 90 per-

Pope John Paul II, in car, visits the Rila Monastery during a four-day tour of Bulgaria in May 2002. The largest monastery in Bulgaria, Rila is also one of the oldest monasteries in all of Europe. (AP Photo/Darko Vojinovic)

cent of Bulgaria's Jews emigrated to the nation of Israel to start a new life. As of 1997, there were only 6,000 Jews living in Bulgaria.

Despite their low numbers, Bulgarian Jews are doing better today than they have in some time. They run their own elementary school, Sunday school, and camp, with aid from foreign donors such as the American Jewish Joint Distribution Committee (JDC). Sofia's Sephardi synagogue has recently been restored. Some Jews that have left for Israel have actually returned. Martin Cohen, 25, returned in 1994. "In Israel, there is no need to preserve your Jewishness because there are Jews all around you," he explained. "Here, we need to save our identity. So whereas in Israel I was an Israeli, in Bulgaria I became a Jew."

Other Religions

The second-largest religious group in Bulgaria are Muslims, who make up about 12 percent of the population. They are mostly ethnic Turks who have lived in Bulgaria for centuries, but they also include Pomaks, Roma

(Gypsies), and Tartars. The vast majority of Muslims live in the northeast and the Rhodope Mountains region.

Of all religious groups, the Muslims probably suffered the most under communism. Persecuted by both the Communists and the Bulgarian Orthodox Church, whose national pride was repulsed by the religion of the Ottoman Empire, the Muslims have enjoyed their own rebirth under a new constitution that upholds religious freedom.

Today there are more than 1,200 mosques in the country. The largest, the Tombul Mosque in Shumen (SHOO-men), which also boasts a theological Muslim school, dates back to 1744.

Roman Catholicism has had to struggle for centuries to be accepted in Bulgaria, where the Bulgarian Orthodox Church has traditionally been strongly opposed to its influence. The Communists viewed the Catholic Church with great suspicion and considered it a pernicious "foreign" influence in the country. Sixty Roman Catholic priests were convicted as Western spies in the infamous "Catholic trials" of the early 1950s; four of them were executed. Relations with the Vatican, first started in 1925, were reinstated in 1990 after the fall of communism. In 1991 there were 44,000 Roman Catholics in Bulgaria, mostly living in the cities of Sofia, Plovdiv (PLOV-dif), and Ruse (ROO-se).

Evangelical Protestants are the fastest growing religious group in Bulgaria today with more than 6,000 members. While Bulgarian Orthodox relations with more mainline Protestant denominations, such as Methodists and Congregationalists, have been friendly since they first arrived in the 1850s, there has been less tolerance shown for the evangelicals. This may be due in part to the fact that some of their most fervent converts have been among the Roma, one of the most persecuted minorities in Bulgaria. In 2001 and 2002, there were several reported attacks by Orthodox groups and young racist skinheads against evangelical Protestants. In 2002 the draft of a denominational law to remove Communist-era restrictions on religious minorities failed to pass in Parliament. Bulgaria still has much progress to make in religious tolerance.

A Land of Superstitions

Centuries of Christianity have not completely eradicated Bulgaria's distant pagan past, and superstitions are still taken seriously, especially by country folk. The same good Christians who attend church on Sunday in rural areas will wear charms to ward off the evil eye when night falls.

Soothsayers and fortune-tellers still hold as much authority for some Bulgarians as the local priest. The most famous of soothsayers was Vangelia Gushterova (van-GE-li-a GOO-shte-ro-va), popularly known as Aunt Vanga, whose death at age 89 in August 1996 was an occasion for national mourning. Blinded in a windstorm of age 12, Aunt Vanga began to have visions of past and future events, many of them with uncanny accuracy. Her humble home in the village of Rupite (ROO-pi-te), south of Sofia, was a shrine to thousands of Bulgarians who often traveled great distances to consult her. Everyone from Communist leader Todor Zhivkov to former president Peter Stoyanov visited Aunt Vanga before making critical decisions. Terminally ill with breast cancer, she refused to be operated on and continued to see Bulgaria's sick and troubled people until shortly before her death. "She lived not for herself but for the people," said former prime minister Zhan Videnov. "That made her a living saint for us."

As Bulgaria struggles to free itself from economic disaster and the shackles of Communist ideology in the 21st century, religion will continue to be a force of both faith and hope.

NOTES

p. 51 "'I say to all . . .'" *New York Times,* May 24, 2002, p. A4.

p. 52 "'There is no doubt . . .'" David Marshall Lang, *The Bulgarians: From Pagan Times to the Ottoman Conquest.* (Boulder, Colorado: Westview Press, 1976), p. 100.

p. 54 "'Now am I truly home . . .'" Naughton, p. 320.

p. 55 "In Israel, there is no need . . ." Jewish Bulletin on Northern California. Available on-line. URL: http://www.jewishsf.com/bk970502/ijews.htm. Downloaded on November 24, 2003.

p. 57 "'She lived not for herself . . .'" *San Diego Union-Tribune,* August 12, 1996, p. B4.

6

THE ECONOMY

Bulgaria's economy has been slowly reviving since the terrible downturn in 1996. By the middle of that year the national economy stood at $12 billion, three-quarters of what it was in 1989. Most banks were insolvent. Inflation was at an all-time high. Foreign debt stood at $9.4 billion. More than 70 percent of the population was living at or below the poverty line. Even the once financially secure middle class was struggling to survive. "We buy only food," said Petar Beron (PE-tar be-RON), a museum curator. "I pay some electricity and heating. Clothes are a thing of the past. It is theoretically impossible to make ends meet in these conditions. You might as well go straight to your funeral. But even to die is not so cheap anymore."

It didn't have to be this way. The Bulgarian people made a critical choice in 1994. Discouraged by hardships intensified by privatization and the reforms necessary to turn the planned market economy of the Communists into a free, open-market economy, the peopled looked to the same Communists, now calling themselves Socialists, to restore stability. But instead of getting better, things only got worse. The Socialists, filled with confidence by their triumphant return to power, stuck to a hard line on the economy. Unlike former Communists in other countries like Poland and Hungary, they remained rigidly ideological and showed none of the political pragmatism that kept reform moving forward elsewhere.

While Prime Minister Zhan Videnov talked about economic reform, his efforts were halfhearted at best. Half a year after the Socialists took over the government, 90 percent of all state-owned businesses were still operated by the state. Many of these companies were inefficiently run and losing money. One computer-disc manufacturer in Pazardzhik (PA-zar-djik) had accumulated $11 million in debt since 1982. But few, from the plant manager to the workers, believed it would close. "We were supposed to be part of the privatization program; now we're going the other way," admitted Felix Domyanov (FE-lix do-MYA-nof), the plant's financial director. "Are they [the government] being honest or not? I've asked myself the same question."

Meanwhile, Videnov refused overtures to work with the World Bank and other international institutions to alleviate the country's massive overseas debts. Given a cold shoulder by the government, dozens of Western businesses and investors left Bulgaria, followed by tens of thousands of young people who could find no job opportunities at home. It was the economic crisis, more than anything, that led to the downfall of the Socialist government in 1997. The right-of-center Union of Democratic Forces (UDF) that came to power in April 1997 went to work immediately to improve the economy. It worked closely with the International Monetary Fund (IMF) to stabilize the currency and reduce inflation. The following year the IMF loaned Bulgaria more than $860 million to initiate economic reforms, including the privatization of state-run businesses, the improvement of social insurance programs, and improvements in agricultural techniques.

By 1998 the gross domestic product (GDP) had risen to $33.6 billion, with a per capita GDP of $4,100. Some 70 percent of state assets had been turned over to the private sector by the conclusion of 1999.

While the UDF made important strides, the economy still lagged behind, leaving many workers unemployed. By 2002 unemployment remained high at 18 percent. The new government of Prime Minister Simeon has continued to work for economic growth, but the results so far have been modest. A $300 million loan from the IMF at the end of 2001 will help the government continue reforms and eventually complete the privatization process.

Before looking at other efforts being made to solve the problems of the Bulgarian economy (see chapter 10), let us examine what role industry, agriculture, and natural resources have played in that economy in the past and the present.

Industry

When the Communists took over Bulgaria in the late 1940s, heavy industry barely existed there. While some light industry flourished, especially textile manufacturing and food processing, 80 percent of the people made their living off the land. It was often a miserable living at best, with small farmers using farming techniques that had changed little since the Middle Ages.

The Communists built factories and industrial plants, creating new heavy industry, often at the expense of light industry. By the late 1980s half of Bulgaria's net material product (NMP) came from industry in which one-third of the nation's workers were employed.

The state ran nearly all businesses, and while everyone who wanted a job had one, management was poor and operations were wasteful. However, as long as the Soviets helped to keep the Bulgarian economy afloat, the people were generally content. As bad as things might be, Bulgarians' standard of living was generally better than it had been before. But as communism weakened in the 1980s and the Soviet Union's economy began to flounder, it had a ripple effect in Bulgaria. The Soviet Union had its own problems to deal with, and Bulgaria was ill equipped to build a strong economy independent of its "Big Brother."

With the collapse of the Communist government, new leaders, looking to Western reforms, began the difficult transition toward a market economy. But the slowness of reform and the "shock therapy" of withdrawing state subsidies that people previously relied on quickly soured the public to the new leadership. The former Communists who returned to power were no better at improving the situation. "We haven't had a Leszek Balcerowicz or a Vaclav Klaus [two astute economic architects in Poland and the Czech Republic]," laments one worker. "In Bulgaria, we have only the firm hand of Zhan Videnov—and we see where that is leading us."

Traditionally, the Soviets encouraged heavy industry—the manufacture of machines, trucks, ships, and tools. To diversify and make Bulgaria less reliant on other countries for consumer goods, the early post-Communist governments supported lighter industry, new technology such as electronics and biotechnology, and foreign investment, especially from the West. The Socialists halted most of these efforts, and the new Simeon government is working to restart the process of serious economic reform.

Agriculture and Natural Resources

More than half of Bulgaria is farmland, and it produces a rich array of crops. In the last years of communism, about a fourth of workers were employed in agriculture, providing a fifth of the country's net material product. Just as industry remained stuck in the state's grip in 1996, transfer of the 90 percent of state-run farmland to private farmers progressed painfully slowly at first. By 2001, however, there were 2 million private farms in the country. Unfortunately, only a tiny fraction of them were cul-

THE VALLEY OF ROSES

A rose by any other name would smell as sweet, playwright William Shakespeare wrote. But few roses in the world are as prized for their fragrance as those that have been grown in central Bulgaria's Kazanluk (ka-zan-LOOK) Valley, better known as the "Valley of Roses."

One variety of rose, the pink Damask, is grown not for its blossoms, but for the oil it contains. This oil, known as *attar*, is what gives the flower its fragrance. Attar of rose can be extracted from the blossoms and is a vital ingredient in fine perfumes, cosmetics, soaps, and medicines used to treat patients with respiratory diseases.

Bulgarian attar is the most prized by perfume makers for its uniquely pungent and long-lasting fragrance. The Valley of Roses alone produces about 75 percent of the world's total production of attar. Obtaining the rose oil from the flower is a delicate and painstaking task.

During the harvesting season in late spring the 75-mile (121-km) valley literally becomes a sea of roses. The rose gatherers, many of them schoolchildren, must begin work before sunrise, when the blossoms are moist with dew and the hot sun has not evaporated their oil. The gatherers pick the oily petals and place them in baskets tied to their waists. The petals are then quickly taken to the perfume distillery where they are boiled in water to make the oil rise to the surface. It takes more than 200 pounds of rose petals to produce just one ounce of attar, explaining why the substance and the perfume made from it are so expensive.

The annual Festival of Roses held at the start of the petal-picking season in June draws tourists from the world over. Women and children wear their folk costumes and wreaths of roses. A Rose Queen is selected and presides over dancing, singing, musical concerts, plays, and a

tivating 65 percent of the arable land. The great number of small farms has resulted in low productivity. To counteract this, the Bulgarian parliament passed the Land Consolidation Bill in 2001, which will facilitate creating larger farms from small ones to make them more productive and profitable.

There are two main agricultural regions in Bulgaria. The first is in the north on the Danubian Plateau. Here wheat is grown, Bulgaria's most important cash crop, as well as other grains, sugar beets, potatoes, and sunflowers. Sunflower seeds are fed to livestock, as are the tall stalks that make excellent fodder. The seeds are also crushed for oil used in cooking

parade of flowers. People wander through bright bazaars and arts and crafts exhibitions, eating jams made from rose petals and drinking rose petal brandy. In this valley roses are more than a livelihood—they are a way of life.

These rose pickers in Bulgaria's Valley of Roses work in traditional folk dress. The rose petals must be picked in the early morning before their oil has evaporated in the hot sun. The oil, known as attar, is used in perfumes and other products. (Courtesy Free Library of Philadelphia)

or are roasted and eaten as a snack. The growing season on the plateau is long enough to raise apples, pears, and other fruits.

The second agricultural region is the Maritsa (ma-RI-tsa) River Valley in the south, where the more temperate conditions allow farmers to raise rice, cotton, grapes, watermelon, and tobacco. The grapes are used to make some of the most prized wine in Eastern Europe. Bulgaria's vast vineyards make it the seventh-largest wine-producing nation on earth.

Bulgaria is the world's fourth-largest exporter of tobacco, and Bulgarian cigarettes—with brand names like Shipka, Stewardess, and BT—are sold throughout Europe. Growing tobacco is hard work, as American writer Boyd Gibbons discovered when he joined Vangalia (van-GA-li-a), the wife of the family he was staying with, and other villagers in planting the crop one spring day in the Bulgarian village of Gorna Sushitsa:

> Vangalia coils her braids on top of her head and wraps them with a white *kurpa* [KUR-pa] [scarf]. We bend at the waist, a pile of plants in one hand, and with our thumbs stuff them in the mud a few inches apart. The mud is grainy, camouflaging sharp rocks, and my thumb is soon without cuticle, without feeling. Most of the villagers are out here on the hillsides punching in tobacco or hoeing, their conversation occasionally punctuated by the kibitzing of nightjars [nocturnal birds]. An Italian mower is cutting the hay, but most of the fields are too steep for anything but a *motika* [mo-TI-ka] [a heavy hoe] and muscle.
>
> Walking home that evening, Vangalia smiles and says, "City girls are like eggs—they spoil in the sun. They have learned a lot, but they cannot endure this." Casually I touch my tender back, distinctly feeling the cracking of eggshells.

Just as much hard work goes into the cultivation of roses—which produce Bulgaria's most precious commodity, rose oil, known as attar, used to make some of the world's finest perfumes (see boxed feature).

Among livestock, the sheep is king. There are about 9 million head of sheep, more than the country's human population. These animals are raised for their wool and meat. Pigs and chickens are also common, while bees are kept for their honey, which is used in making many a Bulgarian dish and dessert.

These shepherds are selling wool in the local marketplace. Sheep are the most important livestock raised in Bulgaria. (Courtesy Library of Congress)

Timber from the mountains is a leading natural resource, but Bulgaria has little mineral wealth. Coal, copper, manganese ore, lignite, sulfur, and zinc are mined, but the deposits are small. Oil is also scarce, but in recent years a promising oil industry has been developing on the drilling sites of the Black Sea shelf in the cities of Varna (VAR-na) and Burgas (bur-GAS).

Another important source of power is Bulgaria's swift-running rivers. Hydroelectricity now accounts for a quarter of all electrical power. A nuclear power plant built at Kozloduj (koz-lo-DOOI) by the Soviets pro-vides half of all electricity for the country, but is unsafe (see chapter 10). Although these alternative sources of power help, Bulgaria continues to be plagued by fuel and energy shortages, as the last gas crisis dramatically illustrated.

Banking and Currency

The National Bank of Bulgaria is the principal bank of issue in the coun-try and handles government funds. Private banks were emerging in the early 1990s, but a 1996 banking crisis drove many of them into bank-ruptcy the following year. Today state banks are slowly being privatized.

The monetary unit in Bulgaria is the *leva*. Since 1997 denominations of banknotes from 20 to 50,000 leva have been placed in circulation. Bulgaria is a member of the International Monetary Fund (IMF), which has loaned the country money to stimulate the economy, most recently $300 million at the end of 2001.

Trade

Bulgaria's prospect for international trade received a big boost when it entered the EU on May 1, 2004, along with nine other countries. Full membership is promised by 2007. In the meantime, its main trading partners are Italy, Russia, and Germany. Italy is the leading export partner, followed by Turkey and Germany. Bulgaria's leading exports include clothing, iron and steel, machinery and equipment, and footwear. Bulgaria's leading import partners are Russia, Germany, Italy, and France. Leading imports are minerals, fuel, metals and ores, food, textiles, and chemicals.

Tourism

During the Communist era, Bulgaria was a major tourist destination for many Soviet Bloc countries. In the decade and a half since communism's fall, this market was lost due to poor management and a difficult economic transition. Today tourism is one of Bulgaria's biggest businesses. In 2002 the tourist industry brought in $1.3 billion. This new tourism market has been driven by Western travelers, who have discovered Bulgaria's great natural beauty, many historic sites, and cheap (by Western standards) prices. It is rapidly becoming one of the most desirable vacation spots in Eastern Europe.

For the past five years, more than 15,000 U.S. peacekeepers stationed in the neighboring republics of Bosnia and Kosovo have spent their furloughs at Bulgarian ski resorts and beaches on the Black Sea. As one visiting American journalist put it, "Bulgaria may have suffered from underdevelopment and bad industrial planning, but its untouched hills and fields may prove to be a blessing for eco-tourism."

Much work needs to be done, however, to develop better tourist facilities and recreational complexes at both the mountains and the seashore. Several ambitious projects, such as a $100 million ski resort and rec center in the Western Rhodopes currently under construction, need an infusion of American and European capital to be completed.

The start of the 21st century is both an exciting and fearful time for the Bulgarians as they rush forward to join their neighbors on the road to economic stability and eventually, it is hoped, prosperity.

NOTES

p. 59 "'We buy only food . . .'" Tracy Wilkinson, "Corruption and Poverty Freed Rebellion in Bulgaria," *Los Angeles Times*, January 23, 1997, p. A1.

p. 60 "'We were supposed to be part . . .'" *Washington Post*, July 7, 1996, p. A21. CD NewsBank.

p. 61 "'We haven't had a Leszek Balcerowicz . . .'" *Washington Post*, July 7, 1996, p. A21. CD NewsBank.

p. 64 "Vangalia coils her braids . . ." Boyd Gibbons, "The Bulgarians," *National Geographic*, July 1980, p. 104.

p. 66 "'Bulgaria may have suffered . . .'" *New York Times*, September 23, 2001, pp. TR 6–7.

7

CULTURE

The Bulgarians have a right to be proud of their culture. As author Emil Georgiev (e-MIL ge-or-GI-ef) writes: "[they] were among the first [in Europe], after the decline of the ancient world, to found their own state and launch their own culture." Although Bulgaria's golden age of the arts ended early in its long history, culture has remained a safe refuge from the invading hordes over the centuries and has kept the flame of the people's spirit alive through dark times. It is a culture that is uniquely democratic, meant to be enjoyed by all people, whether it is expressed in a poem praising the Bulgarian countryside, a church icon, or a folk song.

Language

The Bulgarian language was the first true Slavic tongue, and its history is deeply rooted in Slavic civilization. A pair of learned brother monks, saints Cyril (SER-il) (ca. 827–869 A.D.) and Methodius (ma-THO-dee-us) (ca. 825–884 A.D.) created the Cyrillic (ser-IL-lik) alphabet to help found a Slavic church in Moravia, part of the present-day Czech Republic. The church did not survive, but the alphabet did. It was brought to Bulgaria by the two monks' disciples and gave birth to the Bulgarian language. From there the Cyrillic alphabet spread throughout the Slavic lands.

Bulgarian is closely related to Russian, although its grammar is somewhat different from other Slavic languages, and in some ways resembles English. The language was banned under the Turks and became a tool for Bulgarian nationalism in the 19th century. It helped create a new contemporary literature that flourished after independence in 1878.

While Bulgarian is the official language of more than 8 million Bulgarians, it is not the only language spoken in the country. Ethnic minorities also speak Turkish, Armenian, and Greek in the regions where these people have settled.

Literature

Bulgaria's golden age of literature flourished during the reign of Simeon I and the First Bulgarian Kingdom. Monks and other scholars turned out great religious and secular literature that spread Christianity and Slavic culture throughout Eastern Europe. When the first Bulgarian Kingdom collapsed early in the 11th century, the Byzantine Empire took power and foisted its own culture on Bulgaria. Bulgarian literature went "underground," returning to the villages and towns where it was kept alive in countless folktales, heroic sagas, proverbs (see boxed feature in chapter 9), riddles, and songs. This was primarily an oral tradition, and the first Bulgarian book published in Cyrillic did not appear until 1651 in Rome.

Father Paisiy of Hilendar's *History of Slavo-Bulgarians* (1762) was the beginning of the national revival that reached its peak in the early 19th century. Writers and intellectuals not only wrote books but opened schools for Bulgarian children, published newspapers and textbooks, and collected folktales from the countryside—all in their native language.

Chitalishta (chi-TA-li-sta), a network of public reading rooms open to all, first appeared in this period. More than mere reading rooms, they were intellectual and cultural centers where common people could meet, take classes in the arts, and even put on plays for the community. The chitalishta established the importance of the arts in a nation that was rediscovering itself and its culture. They remain an important part of literary and intellectual life in Bulgaria today.

The most-read author of the nationalistic period was Ivan Vazov, often called the "father of modern Bulgarian literature." His most celebrated work is *Under the Yoke* (1888), a fervid, patriotic novel about Bulgarian society on the brink of the April Uprising of 1876 against the Turks. It is one of the few Bulgarian novels that has been translated into many languages including English. Vazov is best known for this and other historical novels, but he also wrote stories, poems, and plays. His collected works fill over a hundred volumes.

As in many European countries, writers in Bulgaria in the early 20th century moved away from realism, a literary movement that pictures life as it actually is. Poets wrote a new kind of symbolist poetry filled with strange poetic images of death and decay. War and displacement haunted young writers like Dimcho Debelyanov (DIM-cho de-be-LYA-nof) (1887–1916), who expressed his love for his war-torn country in melancholy but beautiful verse. Debelyanov volunteered to fight in World War I and was killed in action.

Many Bulgarian writers were willing to fight and, if necessary, die for their country, but when the Communists took over, they discovered that an even sturdier heroism was needed. Life became a daily struggle to express themselves under what one writer calls "a Stalinist straitjacket." The writers who refused to become part of the Communists propaganda machine were arrested, tried, and either executed or sentenced to labor camps. Some chose suicide over living under such a repressive government. The poet Yosif Petrov (YO-sif pet-ROF) (b. 1909) was deprived of pen and paper in a labor camp and was forced to write poems in his head during these difficult years. He later recalled these prison poems and wrote them down for publication.

Another brave Bulgarian writer, Georgi Markov, fled his homeland and settled in England, where he wrote such stinging critiques of the Communist regime as *Reports from Bulgaria from Abroad* and *The Truth That Killed*. Assassinated by Bulgarian Communist agents, Markov was posthumously awarded the Order of Stara Planina, Bulgaria's highest honor, in December 2000.

The Bulgarian writers who stayed home and continued to write what was on their mind often eluded censorship by hiding their message in folklike fables and coded poetry. Among the most outspoken dissident writers in the 1960s was Blaga Dimitrova (BLA-ga di-mi-TRO-va) (b. 1922), whose poetry and prose attacked the corruption of the Communist system. In this excerpt from her novel *Journey to Oneself* (1965), she mocked the very language of the Communists:

Collective! The endless speeches, reports, articles, interviews have planted that word in my mind—a parasite which I am powerless to uproot. What was "collective" about our life in that hut? We shared no common purpose, no common interests, no common rhythm. They tried to unify us through the medium of competitions: for the best kept room, the punchiest slogans, the brightest decorations. We were unimpressed.

While such writing did not get Dimitrova's work banned, a number of her books were not allowed to be published in Bulgaria. But her courage gained her an admiring public, and in 1990, with the collapse of communism, she was elected a member of the National Assembly. In January 1992, at age 70, Blaga Dimitrova was elected vice president of Bulgaria, the first woman ever to hold so high an office in the government. She fought hard for issues affecting children and women, as well as the rights of minorities such as the Turks. Frustrated by the political process, Dimitrova resigned in 1994.

Another leading contemporary writer is Anton Danchev (b. 1930), whose novel *The Strange Knight of the Holy Book* won the prestigious Balkans literary prize the Balkanika in 1998. Danchev is also a leading screenwriter of film and television.

Today Bulgarian literature continues to speak out against injustice, but ironically, the lack of government support for literature and the arts in the new Bulgaria has made it difficult for many writers to get their works published.

Music

Music and singing come as naturally to most Bulgarians as breathing. The country's rich heritage of folk music goes back to earliest times, but it continues to be an important part of Bulgarian life today. "It reflects, along with fragments of past history and extinct religion, the everyday life of thousands of villages . . . good luck and bad, love, quarrels and death in such an intimate way, sometimes humorous, sometimes tender but always tense and vivid. . . ." writes author Elizabeth Marriage Mincoff in her book *Bulgarian Folksongs.*

The Bulgarian folk song has gained international acclaim through such touring groups as the Bulgaria A Cappella Choir and the all-women

LJUBA WELITSCH (1913–1996)

Bulgaria has produced many great opera singers. Perhaps no Bulgarian singer made a more spectacular debut in the world of opera than did soprano Ljuba Welitsch.

Welitsch was born in Borissova (bo-RI-so-va), a town on the Black Sea coast. A singer and violinist from childhood, she first sang professionally in 1936 for the Graz Opera Company. After singing many roles in German opera houses, she made her debut at the Vienna Opera in the starring role of Salome, the homicidal stepdaughter of King Herod in Richard Strauss's daring modern opera *Salome* in 1944. Strauss himself praised her performance, and the role became her favorite.

She was engaged by the Metropolitan Opera House in New York in 1949 to sing Salome and stunned the opening night audience with her acting and singing talent. One reviewer in the *New York Times* called her "an actress of individuality and power," as well as a great singer. The performance remains one of the most memorable in the history of that great opera house.

In the five years following *Salome,* Welitsch sang so much that she nearly ruined her voice and could no longer sing starring roles. However, she continued to sing less demanding roles and act in films, recordings, and onstage into the 1980s.

In 1956 she created a stir in the newspapers when at age 43 she married a 29-year-old traffic police officer who had helped her after an automobile accident. An extravagant woman who did nothing halfheartedly, Welitsch always lived up to her name, which in Bulgaria means "love great."

Bulgarian-born opera singer Ljuba Welitsch took the international world by storm in the 1940s with her stunning performance as the seductive Salome, in the opera of the same name. (Courtesy Free Library of Philadelphia)

Bass opera singer Boris Christoff cuts a forceful figure in his signature role of Czar Boris Godunov in the acclaimed Mussorgsky opera of the same name. (Courtesy Free Library of Philadelphia)

chorus Le Mystère des Voix Bulgares.

Almost as much loved as folk music is opera. The country boasts five opera houses and a number of great opera singers, especially bassos, who have gone on to international fame. Boris Christoff (bo-RIS HRIS-tof) (1914–93) was best known for his unforgettable portrayal of the tortured czar Boris Gudonov in the Russian opera of the same name, and Ljuba Welitsch (LYOO-ba VE-lich) (see boxed biography) is remembered for her striking interpretation of the seductive and dangerous princess in *Salome*. Other Bulgarian-born opera singers who have achieved celebrity beyond Eastern Europe are Nikolai Ghiaurov (ni-ko-LAI gya-OO-rof), Raina Kabaivanska (RAI-na ka-BA-i-van-ska), and Ghena Dimitrova (Ge-na di-mi-TRO-va).

One of Bulgaria's leading contemporary composers is Bozhidar Abrashev (b. 1936). A noted professor of music at the state music academy for more than three decades, Abrashev has composed 60 works, including symphonies and choral pieces. In 2002 he was named Bulgaria's minister of culture. In this position he is an ardent advocate for the arts in national life.

Bulgaria has 12 symphony orchestras, including the Sofia Philhar-monic and the Bulgarian National Radio Symphony, both of which per-form during the annual Sofia Music Weeks from May 24 to July 2.

Bulgarian instrumental folk music is rich in rhythms and highly sophisticated meters and beats. The music is played on such unusual folk instruments as the *gaida* (GAI-da), a kind of bagpipes; the *kaval* (ka-VAL), a wooden flute; and the *gadulka* (ga-DOOL-ka), a stringed instru-ment played with a bow that resembles a mandolin. The most popular Bulgarian folk dance is the *horo* (ho-RO), where dancers swirl around in a circle, holding hands.

Art

Bulgarian art is less known to the outside world than is its music, but it has an equally impressive breadth and range.

During the First Bulgarian Kingdom, artists and artisans expressed their faith in gorgeous church murals, frescoes, and small religious images painted on wood called icons. Many of these artworks can be seen today in museums, churches, and monasteries. They bear the strong influence of Byzantine art, especially in their dark, vibrant colors.

Two of the most famous of 20th-century Bulgarian artists are concep-tualist Christo (HRI-sto) (see boxed biography), who now lives in the United States, and painter Zlatyo Boyadziev (ZLA-tio bo-ya-DJI-ef) (1903–76), who lived and worked in Plovdiv. Boyadziev suffered a stroke in 1951, which affected his brain and the way he saw colors. His painting style changed dramatically, and his later paintings are, in the words of one critic, "explosions of color, dazzling and highly evocative." A special exhibit of Boyadziev's work was held in Sofia on the 100th anniversary of his birth in 2003.

Another contemporary artist who, like Christo, now lives in the United States, is painter Antonia Toneva, whose earlier career as a com-puter artist has heavily influenced her paintings. One of her recent accomplishments is an ambitious multimedia work made up of 30 large canvasses that are painted in sequence like a movie. "Art is more than life for me," Toneva has said. "It is the uniting of life, death, eternity, and the meaning of human existence."

CHRISTO (b. 1935)

While other artists paint pictures or create sculptures, the Bulgarian-born artist known as Christo sees the whole world as material for his art. Since the early 1960s, this controversial artist has been leaving his eccentric mark on the landscapes of a dozen countries—a curtain dropped across a rugged valley in Colorado, giant umbrellas in Japan, the German Reichstag (a government building) wrapped in more than a million square feet of silver polypropylene fabric. His masterpiece may be a 24-mile (39-km) fabric "fence" running along a stretch of California coastline.

He was born Christo Javashev (ya-Va-shef) in Gabrovo (GA-bro-vo), Bulgaria, where his father was a chemist and businessman. He attended Sofia's Fine Arts Academy and was studying in Prague, Czechoslovakia, in 1956 when the Hungarian Revolt broke out and was quickly crushed by the Soviets. Christo fled to the West to escape communism and eventually settled in Paris, where he made sculptures out of bottles and cans.

One of his first large-scale works was called *Iron Curtain—Wall of Oil Drums*, which were just that. He set it up on a Parisian street where it blocked traffic.

In 1964 Christo moved to New York City with his French-American wife and collaborator, Jeanne-Claude. In New York their projects grew more and more grandiose. Some were too outlandish to actually complete, such as their plan to erect 48-foot (15-m) high glass walls on every east-west highway in the United States. But others have been completed at enormous effort and cost, such as the covering of a 1-million-square-foot section of the Australian coastline with erosion-control fabric and 36 miles (58 km) of rope. Over a quarter century of work will reach

Those artists who have chosen to stay in Bulgaria have found it difficult to support themselves in an unstable economic system.

While the Communists funded artists who painted in the realistic style they approved of, artists who refused to compromise their vision could still get funding for state-commissioned murals and other public works of art. In post-Communist Bulgaria, ironically, that has all changed. "For the fine artists there is no structure of support," complains artist Ilia Petkov (i-LI-ya pet-KOF). "Private funds go after cheaper artists

its completion in 2005, when 7,500 saffron-colored gates will cover 23 miles (37 km) of pedestrian walkways in New York City's Central Park. Some people think Christo's work is silly and a waste of money and resources, while others see it as brilliant commentary on the natural and human-made world we live in. Christo biographer Burt Chernow opined that "to be in the presence of one of these artworks is to have your reality rocked. You see things you have never seen before."

Bulgarian-born artist Christo and his wife and close collaborator, Jeanne-Claude, proudly accept the Rosenthal Award of 2000 for lifetime achievement in design in Frankfurt am Main, Germany. (AP Photo/HO)

Christo himself sees both the obstacles and the triumphs as a part of each of his works. "For me esthetics is everything included in the process—the workers, the politics, the negotiations, the construction difficulty. . . . I'm interested in discovering the process. I put myself in dialogue with other people."

and look to support touristic artwork. I thought I was ready for the opportunities of democracy. Now I find I'm not prepared. . . ."

Theater

The theater is an integral part of Bulgarian life and culture. From the national theater in Sofia, established by the Communists, to the smallest village production, theater, like the other arts, belongs to the people.

During that National Revival of the 19th century, theater was meant to rouse Bulgarians' feelings of patriotism and nationhood. In his novel *Under the Yoke*, Ivan Vazov describes with insight and humor the reactions of simple village folk to a local production of a stirring patriotic drama:

> Then came the third act. . . . Golos appears, dishevelled, ugly, tortured by remorse and wearing the fetters of the konak* [ko-NAK] prison. He is greeted by a hostile murmur from the audience. Angry looks pierce him. The Count reads him a letter in which the Countess includes him in her forgiveness, and breaks down again, tearing his hair, beating his breast. The audience sobs again unrestrainedly.
>
> Aunt Ghinka is also shedding tears, but wants to reassure the others. "There's nothing to cry about, Genevieve is alive in the forest!"
>
> Some of the old women, who don't know the play, speak up in surprise. "Heavens, Ghinka, is she really? Why don't somebody tell him, poor man, and stop him crying?" said Granny Petkovistsa, while Granny Hadji Pavlyuvitse, unable to restrain herself, called out through her tears, "There, my boy, don't cry; your bride's alive!"

In the Communist era, playwrights and their audiences became more sophisticated. They used satire, disguised in the form of simple parables, to attack the repressive political system they lived under. The contemporary playwright, short story writer, and novelist, Yordan Radichkov (yor-Dan ra-DICH-kof) (b. 1929) has had his plays performed in Western Europe and the United States. He also writes film scripts.

Film

The cinema got a late start in Bulgaria due to the interruptions of war and other calamities in the first decades of the 20th century. Vassil Gendov (va-SIL- JEN-dof) (1891–1970) directed the first Bulgarian film *Bulgarians Are Gallant* (1915) and the first talking film, *The Slave's Revolt* in 1933. For years he was the only Bulgarian film director and struggled to make his films under difficult circumstances.

---

*The governor's residence, seat of the local Turkish government.

The Communists nationalized and enlarged the Bulgarian film industry, but the films they produced were mostly dull historical epics meant to inspire the Bulgarians to make greater sacrifices for their Communist government. New and imaginative young directors appeared in the late 1950s making films that dealt with serious contemporary issues. Rangel Vulchanov's (RAN-gel vul-CHA-nof) *Sun and Shadow* (1962) and *The Peach Thief* (1964), directed by Vulo Radev (VU-lo RA-def) (1923–2001), were the first Bulgarian films to be widely seen abroad. By the 1970s the Bulgarian film industry was turning out 20 features and 200 short films a year, including many animated works. Since the fall of communism, the industry has taken a nosedive. With limited state funding, many directors have been unable to raise money to make films, and some of Bulgaria's 271 movie theaters have been forced to close.

While the Bulgarian film industry is still very sluggish, there are promising signs. Such popular contemporary filmmakers as Iglika Triffonova (b. 1957) and Kostadin Bonev (b. 1951) continue to make challenging films. Bonev's *Warming Up Yesterday's Lunch* (2002) was Bulgaria's submission for the best foreign film category at the 2003 Academy Awards. The Sofia International Film Fest will celebrate its eighth year in 2004. At the 2003 fest some 120 films were screened, including several from Bulgaria.

Bulgarian culture, one of the most pluralistic in Europe, has been dealt an unexpected blow by democracy. Until Bulgaria is further along the road to a freer system of government and a stable economy, the arts will be just another casualty of the difficult transition from communism to democracy.

"Culture is burning in our part of the world," says artist Ilia Petkov. "But culture will rise from the ashes like the phoenix."

NOTES
p. 69 "'[they] were among the first . . .'" Naughton, p. 290.
p. 72 "*Collective!* The endless speeches . . ." Naughton, p. 319.
p. 72 "'It reflects, along with fragment . . .'" Quoted in Assen Nicoloff, *Bulgarian Folklore* (Cleveland, Ohio: published by the author, 1983), p. 48.
p. 75 "'Art is more than life . . .'" Artists in the Spotlight: Antonia Toneva. Modamag.com Available on-line. URL: www.modamag.com/antonia.htm. Downloaded on November 12, 2003.
p. 76 "'For the fine artists there is no structure . . .'" Eleanor Kennelly, "Pictures etched in his mind," *Washington Times*, January 4, 1996, C8. CD NewsBank.
p. 77 "'to be in the presence . . .'" *Connecticut Post*, February 10, 2002, p. G3.

p. 77 "'For me esthetics is everything . . .'" *Current Biography 1977* (New York: H. W. Wilson, 1978), p. 110.

p. 78 "Then came the third act . . ." Ivan Vazov, *Under the Yoke* (New York: Twayne, 1971), p. 91.

p. 79 "'Culture is burning . . .'" *Washington Times*, January 4, 1996, C8. CD News-Bank.

8

DAILY LIFE

Since communism's fall, daily life in Bulgaria has become more and more of a struggle for survival. The majority of people live in poverty or near poverty. The middle class is virtually nonexistent. Professional people like doctors and lawyers face the same economic hardships as everyone else. The small privileged class that does exist did not get its wealth through education and hard work, but through good connections and corrupt practices. Is it any wonder most Bulgarians look toward the future with cynicism?

Education

Any hope for the future in Bulgaria may lie in its educational system. Education is a top priority in this small country, and school is part of daily life for every child from six to 16.

Under the Communists, children did not only learn in school but on the job, working part-time in factories and on farms at careers they were interested in pursuing. The government adapted schools to accommodate working parents, which included nearly every couple in the country. Students remained after school in study halls called *zanimalnia* (za-ni-MAL-nya) until parents could pick them up on their way home from work. There were even special boarding schools called *internat* (in-ter-NAT) for children whose parents, for whatever reasons, couldn't take care of them.

But if the literacy rate in Bulgaria today is among the world's high-est, at nearly 100 percent, the Communists can take little credit for it. Education has been important to Bulgarians since the early 19th cen-tury. The father of modern Bulgarian education was Dr. Petar Beron (PE-tar be-RON) (1799–1871), a scientist and teacher who immigrated from Romania. In 1824 he published the first school primer in the mod-ern Bulgarian language. Before Beron, schools were modeled on the antiquated monastery system. He created a new, secular model for schools that made education more appealing and intelligible to youth. With the permission of the Turks, a school based on Beron's ideas opened in the city of Gabrovo in 1835. It was the first modern school to teach in Bulgarian.

Today education begins early with four-fifths of all children aged three to six attending preschool. Elementary school goes to the eighth grade, during which time most students begin studying a foreign language, usu-ally Russian, English, or German. High school, called gymnasium, often requires students to pass an entrance exam. Unlike those in the United States, Bulgar-ian high schools are highly specialized. Many of them focus on one area of learn-

Students are on their way to classes at the City University, in Pravets, near Sophia, one of 21 colleges and universities in Bulgaria. (Copyright Valentin Petrovka)

ing—math, science, music, art, public health, or sports. There are also vocational schools that teach students a trade.

The top students from gymnasium go on to one of the 40 institutions of higher learning, which include 21 colleges and universities. The oldest and largest of these is the University of Sofia St. Kliment Ohridski, founded in 1888. Other major universities include The University of National and World Economics in Sofia, the University of Plovdiv, and Sts. Cyril and Methodius University in Veliko Turnovo, the second oldest in Bulgaria.

Despite the variety of institutes of higher learning, there are serious problems. Under communism, a university education was free to those students who qualified. More recently, the government has proposed tuition fees for all students. Many Bulgarians are opposed to these fees. Substandard facilities and poor instruction from Soviet-trained educators are also driving many young people to attend college abroad. Some of them find good jobs in the United States and elsewhere and never return to their homeland except to visit.

Bulgaria is struggling to keep its best and brightest home by improving higher education in a number of creative ways. Standards are being changed to allow more students to enter colleges and universities and pursue a more flexible curriculum. Bulgaria is bringing superior teachers from abroad to teach in its schools. The most outstanding example of this is the American University in Bulgaria (AUBG), in Blagoevgrad, that has an American curriculum and mostly American instructors who conduct all classes in English. In January 2003 AUBG launched the nation's first executive master's of business administration (EMBA) program with 36 students. "The whole idea is to reverse the brain drain," said American Stephen Strauss, the executive director of the Elieff Center for Education and Culture at AUBG. "Rising bright Bulgarian managers who work in the private and public sectors should be able to receive a higher level of education without having to leave the country."

Bulgaria is also pooling its educational resources with neighboring countries. It recently entered into an independent student-exchange program with Greece. Italy allows Bulgarian students to spend up to six months in Italian universities and colleges on a work-study program.

Further proof of the continuing importance of education to Bulgarians is the fact that they have set aside one day each year to honor their

BULGARIAN PROVERBS

WISDOM IN A FEW WORDS

Proverbs are wise old sayings that most Americans relegate to the quaint past. Not so in Bulgaria. Proverbs are a proud part of Bulgarian folk literature that remains very much alive today. People quote proverbs to make a point, support an argument, or just to enliven the conversation. Authors and poets use familiar proverbs in their writing. Parents and teachers use them to teach a moral lesson to children.

Bulgarian proverbs are rich in humor, practical advice, and moral values. With more than 20,000 proverbs in the language, there is a proverb for every situation and occasion. These wise sayings not only help people, but reveal much about the Bulgarian character to the rest of the world.

Many proverbs, not surprisingly, use the language of agriculture. For example: "Every pear has a stem," which means "life is full of opportunity," or "Your mill grinds coarse," which means "You do not attend to your business." Other sayings show how highly the Bulgarians value education: "He who learns will succeed." Still others show a deep respect for age—"An old pot boils tasty broth"—or a certain fatalistic attitude toward life—"The world is a ladder; some climb up, others climb down."

One of the reasons Bulgarian proverbs are so rich in content is that many were borrowed from or influenced by other peoples, including the Turks, the Greeks, the Romanians, the Persians, and the Armenians.

Here are some Bulgarian proverbs and their English equivalents that might sound familiar to you.

Bulgarian	English
Like cow, like calf.	Like father, like son.
Many midwives—a feeble infant.	Too many cooks spoil the broth.
Housework is never at an end.	A woman's work is never done.
Home today, dead tomorrow.	Here today, gone tomorrow.

educators. The Day of Letters (May 24), also known as Education and Culture Day, is a holiday that celebrates learning and knowledge. Students bring flowers to their teachers. Authors and illustrators of children's books read from their works, talk to students, and autograph books. There are exhibits of books and arts and crafts and performances of plays and concerts.

Communications and Media

For an isolated country too long cut off from the Western world, Bulgaria is beginning to make its way into the digital age. In 2001 there were 585,000 Internet users and 200 Internet Service Providers (ISP).

John Atanasoff (1904–95), son of a Bulgarian immigrant to the United States, was a pioneer in digital computing. He built the world's first electronic digital computer at Iowa State University in 1939. Atanasoff's achievement was overlooked at the time, and his reputation was overshadowed by later computer pioneers. Finally, in 1990, Atanasoff was awarded the National Medal of Science and Technology by U.S. president George H. W. Bush. On October 4, 2003, eight years after Atanosoff's death, Bulgarian president Purvanov dedicated a monument to him in Sofia.

There are 3,186,731 main telephone lines (2001 estimate) in operation in Bulgaria and more than a million mobile cellular lines. In June 2003 the Advent International Corporation, a U.S. company, bought more than half of Bulgarian Telecommunications, the state-owned telephone company.

Bulgarians listen to 63 FM radio stations and 31 AM stations. They watch 39 television broadcasting stations. Bulgarians read 11 national daily newspapers and three national weekly papers. Most of these dailies are tabloids that dabble in yellow journalism. The most prestigious daily is *Dnevnik*, while *Douma* is the official newspaper of the BSP. The Bulgarian News Agency (BTA) is the most reliable media agency in the country, founded more than a century ago. Its English-language services are an important source of news about Bulgaria abroad.

Holidays and Celebrations

The Day of Letters is just one of the many celebrations that fill the Bulgarian calendar. In the post-Communist era, the two major Christian holidays, Christmas and Easter, have taken on a greater significance. The Orthodox Christmas is celebrated over three days, from December 24 through 26. Caroling and good eating mark the season. The Bulgarian Santa Claus, Father Frost, doesn't make his appearance until New Year's Day, when he and his helper, Snow White, place gifts under Christmas trees. New Year's Day is the time of another curious custom. Children are allowed to "beat" their elders on the back with decorated dogwood branches. The flowering dogwood symbolizes good health and happiness in the new year. Later, during the New Year's feast, the father or the oldest person in the family lights the yule log, a traditional, large log burned during the Christmas season. The lighting of the log is an assurance of long life. Easter is a more solemn occasion. After church services, families visit the graves of their loved ones and leave flowers.

Other celebrations predate the Christian era and are mostly associated with Bulgaria's rich agricultural past. None is older than Trifon Zarezan (TRI-fon za-re-ZAN), or Vinegrower's Day (January 14), which dates all the way back to Thracian times. Farmers prune their grape vines on this day and spill wine over the shoots to ensure a good growing season. Men of the village march through the streets wearing large grotesque masks and cowbells to frighten away evil spirits. A feast is then held in a meadow with music, drinking, and dancing, all presided over by a local man who has been chosen to be "Vine King."

Shepherds and herdsmen have their holiday, too. On Saint George's Day (May 6), local people and tourists alike flock to the mountains, where lambs are roasted whole over a spit. Traditionally, after the lamb is eaten, some of its bones are buried in an anthill to symbolize that the sheep will multiply like ants. More bones are hurled into the nearest river to signify that lamb's milk will flow like water.

Other holidays commemorate the recent past. National Day of Freedom and Independence (March 3) honors all—both Bulgarians and foreigners— who fought to liberate the country from the Ottoman Turks in the Russo-Turkish War of 1877–78. On Martyr's Day (June 2), Bulgarians remember all who have died in the cause of Bulgarian patriotism. Chief among these is the great national poet Hristo Botev (HRI-sto BO-tef) (1848–76), who died fighting the Turks during the 1876 uprising on June 6.

Sports and Leisure

The Bulgarians are a hardy people, and athletics are an integral part of their lives. Competitive sports began with the Thracians, whose love of wrestling and gymnastics is part of a tradition that continues in Bulgaria today. The drive for athletic excellence can be clearly seen in the country's Olympic record. Bulgaria was one of only 13 nations to take part in the first modern Olympic Games held in Athens, Greece, in 1896. Bulgarian athletes have won numerous medals in track and field, weight lifting, and wrestling. At the 1996 Olympics in Atlanta, Georgia, the world champion Bulgarian women's rhythmic gymnastics team won the silver medal with a spectacular routine using balls and ribbons, put in motion to the sounds of Bulgarian folk music.

Bulgaria's achievement of 13 medals at the 2000 Summer Games in Sydney, Australia, was overshadowed when three Bulgarian weight lifters, including Izabela Dragneva, the first women's gold medalist in the sport, were stripped of their medals after they tested positive for performance-enhancing drugs. Following this, the entire Bulgarian team was expelled from the games. Drug problems continue to dog Bulgarian athletes. In September 2003 rhythmic gymnast Simona Peycheva tested positive for a banned drug at the World Gymnastics Championship in Budapest, Hungary.

In the 2004 Summer Games in neighboring Athens, Greece, Bulgarian athletes will compete in six events: weight lifting, wrestling, rhythmic gymnastics, volleyball, and canoeing/kayaking.

The country's most popular spectator sport, as in many European countries, is soccer. When the Bulgarian soccer team defeated Germany in the quarter finals of the World Cup in 1994 it was a cause for national celebration. Top soccer players are as popular as rock stars are in the United States, none more so than former player Petar Stoyanov, who served as president from 1996 to 2001. Other popular sports are basketball, volleyball, and tennis. Tennis champion Magdalena Maleeva (b. 1975) has been a top international player for more than a decade.

When Bulgarians go on vacation they generally head for one of two locations—the mountains or the seacoast. In the Rhodope and Rila Mountains visitors hike and camp in the summer and ski and toboggan in the winter. At the sandy beaches along the Black Sea coast, vacationers love to swim, fish, or row a boat.

For those too sick or tired to do anything so strenuous there are numerous spas or health resorts surrounding more than 200 mineral springs. Their restorative waters are said to alleviate everything from arthritis to skin disease.

Food and Drink

The Bulgarian national cuisine has been heavily influenced by its neighbors, the Greeks, and former masters, the Turks. Dishes adapted from the Greeks include *sarmi* (sar-MI), stuffed grape leaves; *banitsa* (BA-ni-tsa), a crusty pastry containing spinach and cheese; and *mousaka* (mu-sa-KA), a hash made of lamb and potatoes. Even the most anti-Turkish Bulgarian probably enjoys a morning cup of Turkish coffee, a strong and very sweet beverage. It takes a stronger stomach to drink the alcoholic *boza* (bo-ZA), a thick gray ale made out of fermented grains and *rakia*, a strong fruit brandy.

But there is one popular food that is uniquely Bulgarian—yogurt. This dairy product, made out of cow's or sheep's milk combined with bacteria, was first made here centuries ago. While most Americans eat yogurt as a lunch or snack, Bulgarians eat it at nearly every meal—as a food, a soup, a side dish, or a sauce. They do so for good reasons. Yogurt has been shown to be one of the healthiest of all foods and is even said to prolong the lives of people who make it a regular part of their diet. There may be something to this, for Bulgaria, a nation of yogurt-eaters, has the greatest population of people over the age of 100 in all Europe.

NOTES

p. 83 "'The whole idea is to reverse . . .'" *Wall Street Journal*, March 28, 2003, p. B4 (Eastern edition).

p. 84 "Every pear has a stem," Nicoloff, p. 243.

p. 84 "Your mills grind coarse," Nicoloff, p. 242.

p. 84 "He who learns will succeed," Nicoloff, p. 269.

p. 84 "An old pot boils tasty broth," Nicoloff, p. 256.

p. 84 "The world is a ladder . . ." Nicoloff, p. 263.

p. 84 "Like cow, like calf," Nicoloff, p. 246.

p. 84 "Many midwives—a feeble infant," Nicoloff, p. 254.

p. 84 "Housework is never at an end," Nicoloff, p. 251.

p. 84 "Home today, dead tomorrow," Nicoloff, p. 260.

9

THE CITIES

Not so many years ago cities were a small part of Bulgarian life. The vast majority of people were farmers living in villages and towns. Today that situation has changed drastically. Thanks to the industrialization of the country under the Communists, two-thirds of all Bulgarians now live in urban areas. In 1946, the year a Communist government was installed, there were only two cities in the country that had a population over 100,000—the capital Sofia and Plovdiv. In 2003 there were eight.

Big or small, Bulgaria's cities are survivors. Wars, invasions, fires, and other catastrophes have razed them many times, but they have always risen again, often with new names and new masters. The cities of Bulgaria are a symbol of the resilient spirit of their people.

Sofia: "Ever Growing, Never Old!"

Sofia (pop. 1,088,700),* is Bulgaria's largest city, lying in the foothills of the Vitosha (VI-to-sha) Mountains in the far western region of the country, 1,820 feet (555 m) above sea level. As its motto proudly states, Sofia is an intriguing mix of the old and the new. And "old" means old. Founded nearly 2,000 years ago by the Roman emperor Trajan, it is the second-oldest capital city in Europe after Athens, Greece.

There are many impressive reminders of Sofia's glorious past. The Saint Alexander Nevski Cathedral with its crypt full of priceless icons is

---

*All populations given in this chapter are 2003 estimates.

U.S. president Bill Clinton and then-Bulgarian president Stoyanov wave to a large audience in Alexander Nevski Square in Sofia as fireworks light up the night sky. In the background is Alexander Nevski Cathedral, one of the city's great landmarks. In this November 1999 trip, Clinton became the first U.S. president to visit Bulgaria. (AP Photo/Greg Gibson)

in the oldest part of the city. Nearby is Saint Sophia and another ancient church, Saint George, whose red brick rotunda was built in the fourth century.

While ancient Roman ruins and buildings from later historical periods abound in Sofia, there are fewer reminders left of the recent Soviet past. Lenin's statue and the mausoleum of Communist leader Georgi Dimitrov have been removed. One of the few remaining visible signs of the Soviet era is the ugly blocks of white high-rise apartment buildings that house workers. Many of them have moved from the countryside to work in the city's factories and plants, manufacturing textiles, chemicals, glasses, and electronic goods.

While Sofia's unemployment rate in 2003 was 4 percent, the lowest of any city in the country, there is a segment of the population that has an unemployment rate of about 70 percent. These are the Roma, or Gypsies. Their children, often neglected, make up half of the hundreds of "street children," many of whom spend their days begging, stealing, or selling their bodies as prostitutes. They spend their nights huddled near the heating vents of Sofia's central railway station for warmth in cold weather. This is the underside of Sofia that tourists rarely see.

But Sofia's past has been just as stressful for many of its residents as the present. One of the first invaders after the Romans was the Huns, who destroyed much of the city in about A.D. 450.

The city was rebuilt by Roman emperor Justinian I (483–565), who made it part of the Byzantine Empire and named it Triaditsa (tri-A-di-tsa). The Bulgars conquered the city in 809 and renamed it Sredets (sre-DETS). It soon became the center of Slavic and Balkan culture.

The Byzantines retook the city in 1018 and eventually gave it the name Sofia, in honor of Saint Sofia, whose cathedral was built by the Romans centuries earlier in the heart of the city. Sophia, as the name is spelled in Greek, was the daughter of the emperor Justinian. According to legend, Sophia was incurably ill and her father brought her to the hot springs at the foot of Mount Vitosha, where shepherds cured their sick sheep by submerging them in the restorative waters. Sophia was cured in the same manner, and Justinian built a fortress on the spot to commemorate the miraculous event. It still stands today in the center of modern Sofia.

But no miracle could save the city from the invading Turks, who occupied it in 1382. The Ottomans built their onion-domed mosques alongside Christian churches, changing the skyline of the ancient city forever. Sofia became the residence of Bulgaria's Turkish governors and only became part of a free Bulgaria again in 1878, the year of national independence, when it was also named the new capital.

From a small town of 20,000 souls, Sofia has grown into a metropolis of more than a million people in just a century. Today one in every nine Bulgarians lives in Sofia, and 20 percent of Bulgarian industry is located here.

Sofia is a city of museums and monuments. Besides the great National Museum, there are the Museum of Ecclesiastical History, the Museum of the Revolutionary Movement, the Archaeological Museum, and the National Library. The seat of Bulgarian government and education, Sofia is home to the National Assembly building, the University of Sofia St. Kliment Ohridski, and the Bulgarian Academy of Sciences.

When a visitor wants to sit back and relax amid nature, he or she has some 400 parks to choose from. Several boulevards are paved with glazed yellow bricks that might make visitors think they are on the road to the Emerald City of Oz. This ancient city is keeping an optimistic eye on the future. Sofia is considering a bid to host the 2014 Winter Olympic Games.

Bulgaria's Second City: Plovdiv

Only 90 miles (145 km) southeast of Sofia on the Maritsa River lies Plovdiv (pop. 338,200), Bulgaria's second-largest city. But Plovdiv is second to none in ancient history. An archaeologist's dream, the city has many Roman ruins. The most impressive of these is an amphitheater that once seated 3,000 spectators until Attila the Hun (ca. 406–453) rode through and destroyed a portion of it. Enough of the theater remains, however, to hold concerts and other cultural events each summer. There is also a Roman forum, a restored sacrificial pyre where offerings were burned to appease the gods, two watchtowers and a sixth-century gate, and a good portion of the ancient city walls.

Buildings of more recent times have been put to good use, too. A national revival building from 1847 houses the Ethnographic* Museum, while a Greek Revival building is home to the Archaeological Museum, which contains a stunning collection of Thracian art objects. Another

---

*The science of ethnology deals with different racial or cultural groups of people and their distinguishing characteristics.

fascinating museum is the Museum of the National Revival Period that traces the inspirational story of Bulgaria's final struggle against the Turks.

But Plovdiv also has a more contemporary face, typified by the International Trade Fair held here every spring. Another major event is the International Television Festival held annually in October. The 2003 festival featured 109 productions from 37 countries. Started in 1968 by Bulgarian National Television (BNT) in Sofia, it remains one of the most prestigious festivals of its kind in Europe. Because of its central location, Plovdiv is even more of a transportation hub than Sofia. Textile, food processing, and petrochemical plants dominate its economy, while its medical institute and agricultural school make it an educational center, too. One of the largest wineries in Bulgaria opened in 2003 in the nearby town of Sardinenic.

Varna and Burgas: Cities by the Sea

Bulgaria's 175-mile (282-km) Black Sea coast is a center for tourism, offshore oil drilling, shipping, and fishing. The country's two major ports, Varna and Burgas, are located here.

Varna (pop. 312,300) lies in the north and is Bulgaria's third-largest city and one of its oldest. The oldest known trove of golden objects was discovered here in 1972 (see boxed feature). But today Varna is more rust than gold. State-owned shipyards are rundown and many of the ships are in disrepair. An unnamed party is offering to take over 75 percent of the shipyard's assets, the only way that the shipyard can stay in business and continue to employ its 700 workers.

More profitable are the city's seaside resorts, which are doing a booming business as Western tourists discover their beauty. Varna's cotton textile industry is also doing well, as are the manufacturing of soap, ceramics, foodstuffs, and machinery. Varna was founded by the Greeks in 580 B.C. and named Odessus. In A.D. 679 the Bulgars defeated the Byzantines at Varna in a decisive battle. The Turks seized the city in 1391 and made it a thriving seaport. The last major battle to uproot the Turks from Europe was fought here in 1444 and lost by Polish king Ladislaus III. Varna's location made it an important naval base for the British and French during the Crimean War (1853–56).

THE ANCIENT GOLD OF VARNA

One fall day in 1972 a tractor driver was digging a trench for an electric cable near the city of Varna when he came upon a treasure trove of old bracelets, tools, and squares of shiny yellow sheet metal. When he brought them to Varna's National Museum, archaeologists were amazed to discover that the sheet metal was gold dating back to prehistoric times.

What puzzled museum workers was that no gold objects had ever been found before from this period, known generally as the Copper Age. They were, in fact, the oldest gold objects, to that time, ever found on earth, dating back to possibly 4600 B.C. A full-scale excavation was soon organized, and over the next eight years a total of about 2,000 gold objects were found, including gold necklaces, breastplates, bracelets, and even the gold-encased handle of a stone ax. Most of the objects were part of an ancient cemetery, buried along with the dead to use in the afterlife. Some of the graves contained no bodies but were cenotaphs—monuments in memory of a dead person who is buried elsewhere. These graves contained clay face masks adorned with golden jewelry.

Experts believe the early people who mastered this art of gold making, passed the knowledge on to the Thracians who succeeded them in Bulgaria. "[They] discovered for perhaps the first time in human history," writes archaeologist Colin Renfrew, "the attractive properties—the dazzle, the freedom from corruption, the allure—of that noblest of metals: gold."

Burgas (pop. 192,000) lies further south on the coast. It is Bulgaria's most important fishing port and home of the ocean-going fishing fleet. Since 1991, Burgas's harbor has also been the depository of millions of tons of solid household waste under the supervision of the firm Bulgarian International Services and Investments (BISI). More recently, the citizens of the city have been surprised to discover that BISI is also disposing of huge amounts of industrial waste in their waters, much of it from the former republics of the Soviet Union. The issue has become a controversial one, and public protests may shut down the project. Burgas is a very young city for this ancient land, founded in the 18th century on the site of a 14th-century town. South of the city is a center of petrochemical works, the largest in Bulgaria.

Ruse on the Danube

Bulgaria's chief river port, Ruse (pop. 161,000) lies on the Danube River in northeast Bulgaria, bordering Romania. One of the nation's wealthiest and most sophisticated cities in the 19th and early 20th centuries, Ruse is a sad shadow of itself these days. "It's pleasant enough, with its dilapidated but dignified streets that make it look like a miniature Vienna," notes *New York Times* reporter Richard Bernstein.

Founded in the second century B.C. as Prista, it was used by the Romans as a naval station. In the 19th century Ruse served as Bulgaria's entryway to Europe and was the port for ships carrying goods between the Black Sea and Germany. Still an important commercial and cultural center today. Ruse's greatest tourist attraction may be the childhood home of Nobel Prize–winning author Elias Canetti (1905–94), who wrote lovingly about the Ruse he knew as a child in the memoir *The Tongue Set Free* (1978).

Veliko Turnovo and Gabrovo: Beauty and Laughter

In north-central Bulgaria lie two of the country's most intriguing towns. Veliko Turnovo (pop. 66,500) on the Yantra (YAN-tra) River was Bulgaria's medieval capital and still retains the grace and dignity of a royal city. Here are the ancient fortress on Tsarevets (TSA-re-vets) Hill with its sturdy battle towers and the Holy Trinity Monastery founded in 1070. But what attracts visitors to Veliko Turnovo as much as its history is the natural beauty of the town's surroundings and how they blend in with the buildings. One writer has called it "an entire island of beauty, with whitewashed houses and red-tiled roofs overlooking splendid national revival buildings."

Every summer, Veliko Turnovo is also the site of the International Folklore Festival, which celebrated its seventh year in 2004. It is the biggest event of its kind in the Balkans, featuring nearly 80 folk singing and dancing ensembles from 39 nations.

Gabrovo (pop. 66,900), 30 miles to the south, is also a capital but of a very different kind. It prides itself as the "world capital of Humor." Known for their way with a joke and a funny story, the people of Gabrovo began the world's first Festival of Humor and Satire in 1965. Eight years later the Home of Humor and Satire opened its doors. Statues of movie comic Charlie Chaplin and the humorous but heartbreaking knight Don Quixote stand outside. Inside are rooms full of whimsical artworks from many countries.

There is a more serious side to Gabrovo. It was here that Bulgarian industry began in the early years of the 20th century. Today the city is a major center for textiles, including everything from silk and cotton to buttons and thread.

More Cities Worth Knowing

Each of Bulgaria's cities has its own story to tell. There is Stara Zagora (STA-ra za-GO-ra, pop. 143,000), founded by the Thracians, which was completely destroyed during the Russo-Turkish War and remade as a thoroughly modern city. Stara Zagora is home to two of Bulgaria's most distinguished theater companies. The National Opera Theater, founded in 1928, was the first provincial opera theater in Bulgaria. The State Puppet Theater has an international reputation and has toured Europe and the Middle East. Stara Zagora manufactures about half of all the cigarettes produced in Bulgaria and is near the famous Valley of Roses, which turns out 75 percent of the world's attar (see sidebar, chapter 6).

Pleven (PLI-ven, pop. 121,300) in north-central Bulgaria is an important commercial center whose main industries are cotton textiles and food processing. During the Russo-Turkish War of 1877–78, the Turks defended the city fiercely, finally capitulating to the Russians after four months of fighting. It was a decisive victory for the Russians, leading to the war's end.

Another strategic site during the war was Shumen (SHOO-men, pop. 88,400) in northeastern Bulgaria, named Kolarovgrad from 1950 to 1964 in honor of Communist leader Kolarov (ko-LA-rof), who was born there. Site of the largest Turkish garrison during the Ottoman Rule, Shumen is home of Tombul Mosque, the largest and oldest mosque on the Balkan Peninsula. Konstantin Preslavski University is located here, along with the first Bulgarian theater and orchestra.

The cities of Bulgaria have, like their people, endured many hardships, but they continue to thrive. As more and more Western visitors enter this little-known land for the first time, it is the cities, with their rich past, that are likely to first win their hearts.

NOTES

p. 94 "'[They] discovered for perhaps the first time . . .'" Colin Renfrew, "Ancient Bulgaria's Golden Treasures,'" *National Geographic*, July 1980, p. 129.

p. 95 "'It's pleasant enough . . .'" *New York Times*, September 1, 2003, p. A3.

p. 95 "'an entire island of beauty . . .'" *New York Times*, Travel Section, June 23, 1996, p. 18.

10
PROBLEMS
AND SOLUTIONS

"We are born with tears and with tears we die," says an old Bulgarian proverb. The people of this small, beleaguered country are used to suffering. They have borne much in their long, tearful history, but they have also achieved much. There is a strong practical streak in the Bulgarians that may well help them to persevere and deal with the many problems that will continue to plague them in the years ahead. The new centralist coalition government is earnestly seeking solutions to the problems of the past and present to forge a better future. Here are some of those problems and their possible solutions.

The Economy

After a decade of stagnation and constant problems, the Bulgarian economy is, in many ways, better off today than it has been since the fall of communism. Exports are up, inflation is low, and the tourism industry is booming as Westerners flock to Bulgaria's ancient cities and beautiful countryside. In 2003 the Simeon government predicted that productivity would double within two years.

That's the good news. But there is bad news, too. The average Bulgarian has not yet benefited from the economic upturn. The average monthly salary in 2003 was only 280 leva, about 160 U.S. dollars. Unemployment,

Angry protestors in downtown Sofia call for the government to resign after failing to lower unemployment or improve a plummeting economy. The November 2002 rally of up to 6,000 was organized by labor unions. (AP Photo/Dimitar Deinov)

while low in Sofia and some other urban centers, is still high nationally, about 20 percent. Foreign countries have responded to widespread crime and corruption by cutting aid, investment, and expertise to Bulgaria.

The economic situation should improve with Bulgaria's expected entry into the EU in May 2004, as the country's opportunities for trade greatly increase. But Bulgaria cannot expect EU membership to solve all its economic problems. It must aggressively seek out other economic ties abroad and encourage foreign investment by making it a more desirable location for foreign businesses. One positive move was the signing in October 2003 of a trade and cultural exchange agreement with Ukraine, one of its largest neighbors. "Ukraine is a large market, and in my personal view Bulgaria should be present in it," said Ukrainian president Leonid Kuchma, after the signing with President Purvanov. Kuchma has also offered to help Bulgaria increase its trade with other former Soviet republics in the Commonwealth of Independent States (CIS).

Apathy and Emigration

While the bureaucratic communist system took away people's initiative and made them politically apathetic, the subsequent post-independence governments have done little to increase confidence.

Viktor Pashov, a Bulgarian novelist living in Berlin, Germany, and one of the nation's most severe critics, has chastised politicians for refusing to lead in these difficult times. "Our political leaders want somebody to take us out of the dark," he told a reporter. "They are wondering who will lead the way: Europe, Russia, the United States, someone else. At the same time, the leaders do not trust their own people, ordinary Bulgarians, and that is very frightening."

Political distrust is reflected in voter apathy. In the local fall elections of 2003, experts predict up to 55 percent of all eligible voters in Sofia, many of them young people 25 years and under, will not go to the polls.

Many young people have expressed their displeasure with life in Bulgaria by leaving it entirely. Beginning in the 1990s, a record number of youth, seeing no future for themselves in their homeland, have been going abroad to study and find work in France, Germany, Austria, the United States, and Canada. According to the National Statistics Institute, about 50,000 Bulgarians have emigrated each year since 1995. That is about .6 percent of the population. Bulgaria's net population growth in 2001 was minus 5.1 percent. This "brain drain" has had serious consequences on the country's future.

While it may be too late to convince these emigrants to return, it is still not too late to persuade those who have not yet left to stay. Better educational facilities, such as the American University in Bulgaria (AUBG) in Blagoevgrad, is one way to keep Bulgaria's best and brightest from going abroad for schooling. An AUBG center for graduate studies, paid for by Bulgarian-American businessman Eliot Elieff, is the home of the new 16-month accredited EMBA business program. Many of the 36 students in the program have received tuition assistance from their employers, most of them subsidiaries of foreign companies in Bulgaria. With the expertise and skills they gain from the program, these business professionals can help the economy prosper.

The changes, however positive, will take time and that is something many young people do not have. Until the government takes a strong

A BULGARIAN IN AMERICA

Elena Atanassova (e-LE-na a-ta-NA-sova) loves Bulgaria, but she has no intention of returning there to live. The 29-year-old health care consultant lives in Cleveland, Ohio, and first came to the United States in 1996 to study at Eastern Tennessee State University. She misses her family back in Sofia, but she does not miss the everyday problems of life in Bulgaria.

On a visit home in 2000, Elena wanted to go skiing one day. "My mother kept asking me when I was going to get my bus ticket to the ski area," she says. "I told her I was going to buy the ticket on the Internet. Then I realized that I couldn't do that. This wasn't America." Instead she wasted a day traveling to the ticket office, buying her ticket, and returning home.

"Things are moving in the United States," says Elena. "It's more dynamic. If you choose a direction for your life you can see yourself moving forward. Back in Bulgaria, there are lots of people who don't feel they're moving as fast to where they want to be."

Nevertheless, some of Elena's friends have chosen to remain in Bulgaria to be close to their family and friends. "Some of them are saying things will eventually get better," she says. "But I don't think it's going to happen."

Her parents have little faith in the government of Prime Minister Simeon Saxe-Coburg and supported former prime minister Kostov in the 2001 election.

position of leadership and inspires a sense of national pride and identity in Bulgaria's young people, they will continue to feel like Alexander Kirov, a Bulgarian emigrant who lives in Paris and recently came home for a visit. "I don't belong to this country," he told one reporter. "I have my parents, a few friends. Take them away, and Bulgaria is gone."

Human Rights

While Bulgaria has not experienced the divisive ethnic issues that have led to wars in the former Yugoslavian republics, its human rights record

While she has embraced the American way of life, Elena is proud to be a part of the large Bulgarian community in Cleveland. She attends the local Bulgarian Orthodox Church on religious holidays and participates in special events sponsored by the Bulgarian community. She will continue to go back to visit her family, but plans to stay in the United States. On her most recent visit to Bulgaria over the Christmas holiday 2003, she saw some hopeful signs of improvement in people's lives, but not enough to persuade her to move back.

"This is the only place on earth I know, where people make 200 leva on average and have 400 leva expenses per month. Miraculously, they survive somehow."

Bulgarian-born Elena Atanassova prepares to go out with some American friends to a party on New Year's Eve 2002. She thoroughly enjoys her life in the United States and has no intention of returning to Bulgaria to live.
(Courtesy Elena Atanassova)

since independence is a poor one. Among the most despised and persecuted minorities are Roma, the second-largest minority group in Bulgaria.

Most Bulgarian Roma have given up the wandering life of their colorful past and have settled down in urban slums. There the men are often unemployed and their children wander the streets begging and sometimes stealing. Roma are discriminated against in housing, voting, and other social and political areas. Violence against Roma has become commonplace and often goes unpunished by authorities. In June 2001 a security guard shot and killed two Roma trespassers in Mogila and was not prosecuted. In some cases the police themselves have been guilty of abusing

Roma. A Roma suspect held at a police station in Pelven was tortured with electricity while being interrogated.

Prisoners in general are treated abysmally, living in overcrowded prisons with poor sanitation and substandard food. Prisoners in Varna have gone on hunger strikes to protest conditions. In one Sofia prison, the inmates took off the roof as an act of grievance.

Another group that is neglected is the mentally ill. Experts believe it would take $28 million to renovate the 70 homes for the mentally ill nationwide and make them fit to live in. Among the worst is Podgumer, a dilapidated former monastery 12 miles (19 km) outside Sofia that houses 123 men. The beds are steel cots and the toilets holes in the ground. Unruly inmates are placed in a pen called "the cage." Ironically, a new building has been ready for occupancy since 1997, but awaits furniture and beds that have not yet been approved by government bureaucrats. At least one inmate of Podgumer, 39-year-old Veselin Trendafilov, is content to stay where he is. "In Bulgaria, life is not easy," he said. "That's why I think I am better off here than outside."

Until the government makes a genuine and concerted commitment to improve its human rights record for all its citizens, Bulgaria will continue to be looked upon as a pariah in the European community. And that does not bode well for its future.

Women's Rights

One minority whose rights are often overlooked is women. The government has paid little attention to gender issues, even though women have suffered more in the transition to democracy than have men. The economic turmoil has led long-term unemployment for women to soar to 65 percent. Women at home with children must cope as best they can with less income, high prices, and little assistance from social services. Those women who want to find work outside the home are subjected to discriminatory hiring practices and sometimes sexual harassment. There are no anti-sex discrimination laws in Bulgaria at present to counter such practices. Women are often the victims of crimes. According to Zonta Club, an international women's rights group, every fifth woman in Bulgaria is the victim of spousal abuse, illegal trafficking, or enforced prostitution. Police are often unsympathetic and even hostile to female crime victims.

On the positive side, there are a growing number of women's rights groups. They include Zonta Club, the Bulgarian Women's Union, and the Free Feminist Group. The most influential of these organizations is the Women's Alliance for Development (WAD), which has established the only women's information center service in the country.

Also heartening are the women who have appeared in public life as role models for Bulgarian women. Two women hold positions in the Cabinet of Ministers—Minister of Labor and Social Policy Lidia Shuleva (b. 1956) and Minister of Environment and Water Dolores Assenova (b. 1964). Another role model is the president's wife, First Lady Zorka Purvanova, a researcher at the Bulgarian Academy of Science, who is one of a new breed of Eastern European activist first ladies who refuse to remain in the shadows of their husbands.

The Elderly

Traditionally, Bulgarian families have taken good care of their elders. In a recent survey, less than 1 percent of seniors in Bulgaria live in institutions and not in a household. There is even a holiday in their honor, Elderly People's Day, celebrated on October 1 with parades and other events.

However, in hard economic times the elderly have been among the most neglected segments of the population. With a low national birth rate, the ranks of the elderly have swelled. In 2000 Bulgaria became, along with its neighbors Greece, Germany, and Italy, one of the few countries in the world with more elderly people than young people.

Social services for the elderly are restricted, and pensions are modest. While 42 percent of unmarried elderly people live with a child, many others live alone in poverty and growing isolation. Bulgaria has the fourth-highest suicide rate among elderly men in the world, according to a recent study by the *International Journal of Geriatric Psychiatry*. The government is attempting to reform and improve the social services system so it will focus on better, more personal care within the community.

Crime

Crime and corruption are deeply entrenched in every aspect of Bulgarian life today. Under communism, criminal activity was tightly controlled. With independence and the end of political repression, criminals have been free to return to their activities, often with the compliance and encouragement of corrupt businessmen and politicians. Drug smuggling is one major area of crime. Heroin from Southeast Asia and cocaine from South America passes through Bulgaria on its way to the rest of Europe. Bulgaria is second only to Colombia in the production of counterfeit money. The problem is so severe that the U.S. Secret Service has collaborated with the Bulgarian National Service for Combating Organized Crime to establish the Bulgarian Counterfeit Task Force. Banknotes issued since 1997 feature watermarks, microtext, holographic anti-copy elements, and other protective devices to discourage counterfeiters.

Perhaps the most damaging area of crime is the illegal selling of weapons to other governments, a practice that began in the Communist era. Bulgarian arms sellers have a long-standing reputation for selling everything from assault rifles to explosives to the highest bidder, including such rogue governments as Bosnia, Rwanda, and Iraq. The Bulgarian government, under pressure from the United States and other NATO countries, has begun to clamp down on the arms sellers, but it will take strict enforcement to eradicate the problem.

A 2003 government report on organized crime was sharply criticized by President Purvanov for being incomplete and not examining connections between organized crime and politicians. "Bulgaria will never solve the problem of organized crime without confronting the 'big bosses,'" Purvanov said. While positive about a government plan for establishing a Coordinating Center for Crime Control, he feels strongly that there should be a crime-fighting organization that is independent of government.

Among the most courageous crime fighters in Bulgaria is Anna Zarkova, chief crime reporter for *Trud*, a daily newspaper. Zarkova's investigative reporting has exposed organized crime and led to a personal attack on her. In May 1998 she was standing at a bus stop when an assailant threw sulfuric acid in her face, scarring her and blinding her sight in her left eye. Undaunted by the attack, Zarkova continues to be one of her country's most fearless investigative journalists.

Health and Safety

Bulgaria is not a healthy place to live, especially for the sick, the young, and the elderly. Environmental pollution has increased the incidence of respiratory diseases, cancer, and other illnesses. The infant mortality rate in 2003 was an estimated 13.7 deaths per 1,000 live births, one of the highest in Europe. Life expectancy for men is just over 68 years, ten years lower than most of Western Europe.

Health care is still struggling to recover from the economic blows of the 1990s that virtually wiped out budgets for hospitals and other health facilities. Those hospitals that have not closed have been running on a subsistent level, with patients often having to bring or pay for their own basic medical supplies.

Salaries for doctors and other health-care professionals are scandalously low, even by Eastern European standards. The best Bulgarian surgeons earn about $60 a month. Things were so bad at one point at the Queen Jovanna (ya-A-na), Sofia's most prestigious hospital, that doctors were ordered to send home all but the sickest patients and perform no operations for a time.

A poor diet high in fat and low in nutrition and high rates of cigarette smoking and alcohol consumption have added to already high health risks for

A young Red Cross activist writes "NO AIDS" on her face during a public demonstration. Bulgaria, while facing many health issues, has one of the lowest rates of AIDS and HIV infection in Eastern Europe and wants to keep it that way.

the population. Drunk drivers have exacted a terrible toll in car accidents and fatalities. Nearly 15,000 Bulgarians have died in car accidents between 1990 and 2002.

Some experts say the best solution to the current health crisis is nothing less than massive assistance from abroad with medical supplies and food. The government supports a widening of social services to meet the needs of children and the elderly and a national nutritional surveillance system to cut down on malnutrition and the diseases that accompany it.

One health problem that Bulgaria has so far avoided is acquired immune deficiency syndrome (AIDS). As of August 2003, the government reported only about 450 cases of human immunodeficiency virus (HIV), the virus that causes AIDS, out of a population of about 8 million people. This could change, given the steady spread of HIV/AIDS in the region, and preventative steps have been taken. These include free and anonymous government-funded HIV testing for anyone who wants it.

Environment

Environmental pollution is another major health hazard in Bulgaria. The Communists left a terrible legacy for this country of once pristine natural beauty. They poisoned the land with uncontrolled use of pesticides. They polluted rivers and other waterways with industrial waste and sewage. They cut down two-thirds of Bulgaria's primary forest with unregulated lumbering. Deforestation has deprived such birds as the black vulture and the white stork of their habitats, putting them on the endangered species list.

Humans are also at risk. Factory pollution and motor vehicle emissions dirty the air in Sofia and other cities, while metallurgical works and mining contaminate wider regions with poisonous lead, mercury, and sulfur dioxide. Children, the most vulnerable to pollution's effects, suffer from environmentally induced respiratory diseases and damaged immune systems that make them prey to a host of illnesses.

Perhaps the greatest threat to the Bulgarian environment, however, is from a nuclear power plant that lies 124 miles (200 km) north of Sofia. The Kozloduj nuclear plant, opened in 1974 by the Soviets, has one of the worst safety records among nuclear facilities in the world today.

Minor accidents have partially closed the plant numerous times over the past three decades, causing disruptive power cuts across the country. Bulgaria receives half its electricity from Kozloduj.

There has been a growing movement both at home and abroad to shut Kozloduj down permanently. Observers fear it may create the kind of environmental disaster that occurred in 1986 at the Chornobyl nuclear plant in Ukraine. Two of the Kozloduj plant's four reactors were closed in December 2002. The following month, a government accord with the EU to close the remaining two reactors at Kozloduj by 2006 was overruled by the Supreme Administrative Court. The court's decision was based on a vote in Parliament that ruled the reactors should continue to operate until 2007, when Bulgaria's formal entry into the EU is scheduled to take place. An EU team reviewed the two remaining reactors in November 2003 and found them safe to use.

Much of the opposition to nuclear power and other sources of environmental pollution come from private groups and individuals. In the forefront of the struggle is Albena Simeonova (al-Be-na si-me-O-no-va) (b. 1966), a former science teacher, who established the Foundation for Ecological Education and Training (FEET) in 1991 to raise public consciousness of environmental problems and how to best address them. She has successfully led the fight to prevent new construction of nuclear power plants in Bulgaria. In 1993, Simeonova helped to form an association of Bulgarian environmental groups called the Green Parliament. She was awarded the Green Prize for Europe by a U.S. foundation in 1996.

As Bulgaria enters a new century with new leadership, it is hoped that the government will join the Green Parliament in taking more aggressive action to repair and preserve the environment.

Like a hero in one of its fanciful folktales, Bulgaria has suffered many ordeals and setbacks in its quest for happiness. Slaying the dragon of communism has proved far more difficult than anticipated. A magical conjurer, this dragon has been able to transform itself time and again to escape destruction. The beautiful princess in the castle tower, like a mirage, seems all but unattainable. But if this fabled land of ancient glory and present woe can put aside despair, fear, and apathy, and believe in itself, it can yet grasp its destiny like a shining sword and struggle onward to a well-deserved happy ending.

NOTES

p. 99   "'We are born with tears and with tears we die.'" Nicoloff, p. 272.

p. 100   "'Ukraine is a large market . . .'" Sofia Echo.com Available on-line. URL: http://www.sofiaecho.com/cat.php?catid=23. Downloaded on November 26, 2003.

p. 101   "'Our political leaders want . . .'" Bulgaria Arts. Available on-line. URL: archive.tol.czlitowa/mar00bgl.html. Downloaded on October 16, 2003.

p. 102   "'My mother kept asking me . . .'" Elena Atanassova in an interview with the author, November 25, 2003.

p. 102   "'Things are moving . . .'" Atanassova interview.

p. 102   "'Some of them are saying . . .'" Atanassova interview.

p. 102   "'I don't belong . . .'" novinite.com. Available on-line. URL: http://www.the-bulgariannews.com/view_news.php?id=26878. Downloaded on November 26, 2003.

p. 103   "'This is the only place . . .'" Atanassova interview.

p. 104   "'In Bulgaria, life is not easy . . .'" *Los Angeles Times*, September 7, 2003, p. A16.

p. 106   "'Bulgaria will never solve the problem . . .'" Southeast European Times. Available on-line. URL: http://balkantimes.com/default3.asp?lang=english&page=process_print&article_id. Downloaded on November 14, 2003.

CHRONOLOGY

ca. 4,000 B.C.
The Thracians arrive in present-day Bulgaria and establish their civilization

ca. 300 B.C.
Philip II of Macedonia conquers Thrace

ca. 200 B.C.
The Romans invade Thrace and make it part of their empire

A.D. 330
Roman emperor Constantine moves his capital from Rome to Byzantium, renamed Constantinople

ca. 500
The Slavs settle in Bulgaria

ca. 600
The Bulgars invade Slav land and gradually assimilate with the Slavs to become the first Bulgarians

681
Bulgar Khan Asparuhk establishes the First Bulgarian Kingdom

893–927
Simeon I rules Bulgaria, creating a golden age of art, literature, and trade

1018
Bulgaria becomes part of the Byzantine Empire

1186
Ivan I establishes the Second Bulgarian Kingdom

1300s
The Ottoman Turks invade the Balkans from the Middle East and begin five centuries of rule in Bulgaria

1453
Constantinople falls to the Turks, ending the Byzantine Empire

1762
Father Paisiy of Hilendar writes *History of Slavo-Bulgarians*, a lightning rod for Bulgarian nationalism

1876
The April Uprising, last of the rebellions of the Bulgarians against the Turks, is quelled and the Turks retaliate with "the Bulgarian atrocities"

1877–78
The Russo-Turkish War ends with Bulgaria becoming an autonomous republic within the Ottoman Empire

1908
German prince Ferdinand is crowned king of Bulgaria and begins to industrialize the country

1912
The First Balkan War ends in full defeat of the Ottoman Turks

1913
Bulgaria loses the Second Balkan War against Greece, Romania, and Montenegro

1915–18
Bulgaria sides with Germany and Austria-Hungary in World War I and ends up again on the losing side

1919
The Bulgarian Agrarian National Union (BANU) comes to power under the leadership of Alexander Stambuliski

1923
Opponents stage a coup, and Stambuliski is assassinated

1934
The government is seized by Zveno, a fascist-backed political coalition

1935
Boris III becomes royal dictator of Bulgaria

1941
Bulgaria signs the Tripartite Pact with Germany and Italy and becomes their reluctant ally in World War II

1943
Boris dies under mysterious circumstances. His six-year-old son, Simeon II, ascends the throne

1944
The Soviet Union declares war on Bulgaria and seizes the country

1946
A Communist government headed by Georgi Dimitrov takes over Bulgaria

1949
Dimitrov dies and is replaced by Joseph Stalin's protégé Vulko Chervenkov

1954
Todor Zhivkov is made first secretary of the Bulgarian Communist Party one year after Stalin's death

1962
Zhivkov's rise to power in Bulgaria is complete; he is named premier

1965
A coup against Zhivkov fails

1968
Bulgaria sends troops to assist the Soviets in their invasion of Czechoslovakia

1971
A new constitution solidifies the power of the Communists in Bulgaria

1978
September 7: Bulgarian writer Georgi Markov is assassinated in London

1981
Bulgaria celebrates its 1,300th anniversary as a nation

1984–87
Zhivkov's campaign of forced assimilation for ethnic Turks leads to a mass exodus of more than 300,000 Turks from Bulgaria

1989
November: Five thousand people march on the National Assembly in the largest unofficial demonstration in more than four decades; a week later Todor Zhivkov resigns after 35 years in power
December: The Union of Democratic Forces (UDF), a coalition of 16 political organizations, is formed

1990

January: The Communists agree to negotiations with the UDF. Zhivkov is arrested and charged with crimes against the Bulgarian people

June: The first free and open parliamentary elections in more than 40 years take place and the Socialists, former Communists, win a majority of seats

August: President Petar Mladenov resigns and is replaced by UDF leader Zhelyu Zhelev

1991

October: UDF is the big winner in new parliamentary elections
November: Filip Dimitrov forms a new coalition government

1992

December: The Dimitrov government resigns, a new government is formed by another reformer, Lyuben Berov

1994

September: Berov, also unable to improve conditions, resigns; the Socialist Party wins new elections. Zhan Videnov becomes prime minister

1996

May: Ex-king Simeon II visits his homeland after 50 years of exile
November 3: UDF leader Petar Stoyanov is elected president
December: Videnov resigns as prime minister under a barrage of criticism

1997

January: Demonstrators storm the National Assembly, trapping legislators inside; police break up the barricade in a bloody melee; demonstrations continue for weeks

February: The Socialists agree to step down and new elections are scheduled for April; President Stoyanov appoints a caretaker government with Sofia mayor Stefan Sofiyanski as premier

April: UDF is the big winner in parliamentary elections; a new coalition government is formed under the leadership of economist Ivan Kostov

July: A crash program to stabilize the economy goes into effect and includes tighter government monetary control and the privatization of state banks

August: Bulgarian naval forces participate in NATO's Partnership for Peace military exercises in Ukraine with several other Eastern European countries, Turkey, and the United States

1998

August 5: Todor Zhivkov dies at age 86

1999

August: The mausoleum of Communist leader Georgi Dimitrov in Sofia, a symbol of Communist power, is destroyed

November: U.S. president Bill Clinton visits Bulgaria

2000

December: Writer Georgi Markov is posthumously awarded the Order of Stara Planina, Bulgaria's highest honor

2001

April: Simeon II returns to Bulgaria and establishes the National Movement Simeon II (NMSII)

June: NMSII is victorious in parliamentary elections and forms a coalition government with the Turk Movement for Rights and Freedom (MRF)

July: Simeon Saxe-Coburg is named prime minister

December: Socialist Party leader Georgi Purvanov is elected Bulgaria's third president

2002

May: Pope John Paul II visits Bulgaria

September: President Purvanov visits the United States and meets with Secretary of State Colin Powell

December: Two nuclear reactors at the Kozloduj nuclear plant are permanently closed

2003

March 29: Bulgaria and six other countries are admitted as full members of NATO

October 4: President Purvanov dedicates a monument to Bulgarian-American John Atanasoff, inventor of the first electronic computer

2004

May 1: Bulgaria and nine other nations are admitted to the European Union.

FURTHER READING

NONFICTION BOOKS

Bar-Zohar, Michael. *Beyond Hitler's Grasp: The Heroic Rescue of Bulgaria's Jews* (Holbrook, Mass.: Adams Media Corporation, 1998). The definitive work on how Bulgaria saved its 50,000 Jews during World War II.

Crampton, R. J. *A Short History of Modern Bulgaria.* (Cambridge, England: Cambridge University Press, 1997) A concise survey of Bulgarian history from 1878 to 1996.

Curtiss, Glenn E., ed. *Bulgaria: A Country Study.* Washington, D.C.: Library of Congress, 1993. A comprehensive survey of contemporary Bulgaria, probably too detailed for most young adults, but well worth a perusal.

Markov, Georgi. *The Truth That Killed* (New York: Tickhor & Fields, 1984). The memoir of the Bulgarian writer who was assassinated for his outspoken criticism of the Zhivkov regime.

Resnick, Abraham. *Bulgaria.* Chicago: Children's Press, 1995. A good young-adult introduction to Bulgaria, past and present, part of the excellent Enchantment of the World series.

Stavreva, Kirilka. *Bulgaria.* New York: Marshall Cavendish, 1997. Another good young-adult introduction to the country and people, well illustrated, with the emphasis on culture and society rather than contemporary political events.

Todorov, Tzveton, and Robert Zaretsky, editors. *Voices from the Gulag: Life and Death in Communist Bulgaria* (University Park, Pa.: Pennsylvania State University, 2000). Gripping accounts of life in the Soviet gulag from the people who lived it.

FICTION, POETRY, AND FOLKLORE

Dimitrova, Blaga. *Scars* (Princeton, N.J.: Ivy Press, 2002). A recently translated Collection of poetry from one of Bulgaria's leading poets.

Naughton, James, editor. *Eastern and Central Europe: Traveller's Literary Companion.* Chicago: Passport Books, 1996. Excellent guide and introduction to the literature of Bulgaria and other Eastern European countries, with brief excerpts from the work of important writers.

Nicoloff, Assen. *Bulgarian Folklore*. Cleveland: published by the author, 1983. A comprehensive, academic study of Bulgarian folklore, with many examples of folk beliefs and customs, folk songs, folktales, and proverbs.

Pridham, Radost. *A Gift from the Heart: Folk Tales from Bulgaria*. Cleveland: World Publishing Co., 1967. An enchanting collection of Bulgarian folktales, retold by a writer who was raised in Bulgaria.

Sapinkopf, Lisa, and Georgi Belv, eds. *Clay and Star: Contemporary Bulgarian Poets*. Minneapolis: Milkweed Editions, 1992. An excellent cross section of poets and representative poems, many of them accessible to young adults.

Vazov, Ivan. *Under the Yoke*. New York: Twayne, 1971. The best-known Bulgarian novel in the West, by one of Bulgaria's most-beloved authors. It portrays events in one village leading up to the 1876 April Uprising against the Turks. Vazov's characters are two-dimensional, his plot contrived and melodramatic, but the insights into Bulgarian village life near the end of Turkish rule are intriguing.

WEB SITES

Bulgarian News Network. Available on-line. URL: http://www.bgnewsnet.com. An excellent daily newspaper with backlog of related stories to put latest news into perspective.

Novinite.com. Available on-line. URL: http://www.thebulgariannews.com. A daily news digest including business and political news and various features.

Sofia Echo.com. Available on-line. URL: http://www.sofiaecho.com. A weekly news magazine with extensive archives of back issues.

INDEX